INKY DINKY DOODLE COLORING BOOK

Cheri Pellegrino Khorram

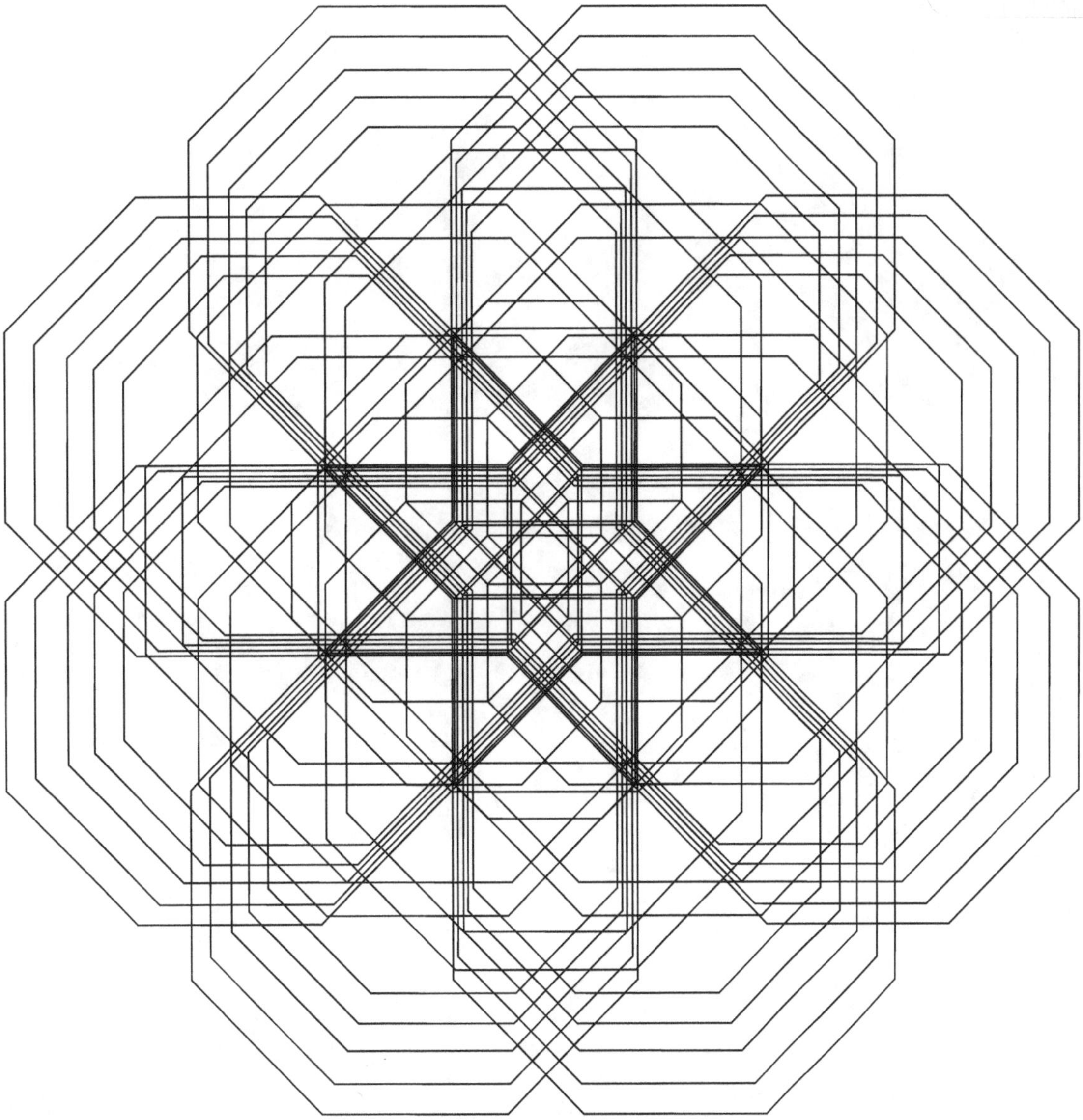

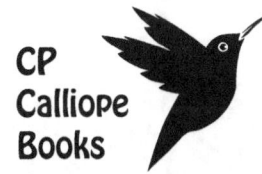

CP
Calliope
Books

GEOMETRICS

To Kerri, I love you. -C.P.K.

We'd love to hear from you! Send your questions, comments, and even your artwork to info@CheriPK.com.

We'd love to see what you created with our coloring book. We may post your colored creations on our Facebook page, so send one design or send them all!

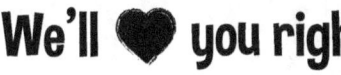

Facebook Page - http://www.facebook.com/CheriPK.art
Website - http://www.CheriPK.com

Send Us Some Lve!
Leave us a review on Amazon.
We'll ❤ you right back!

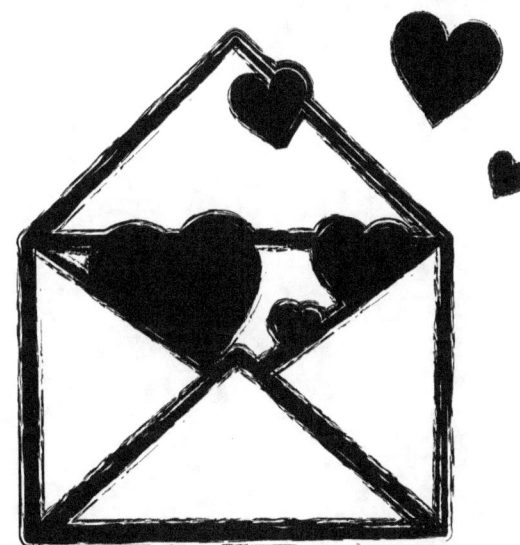

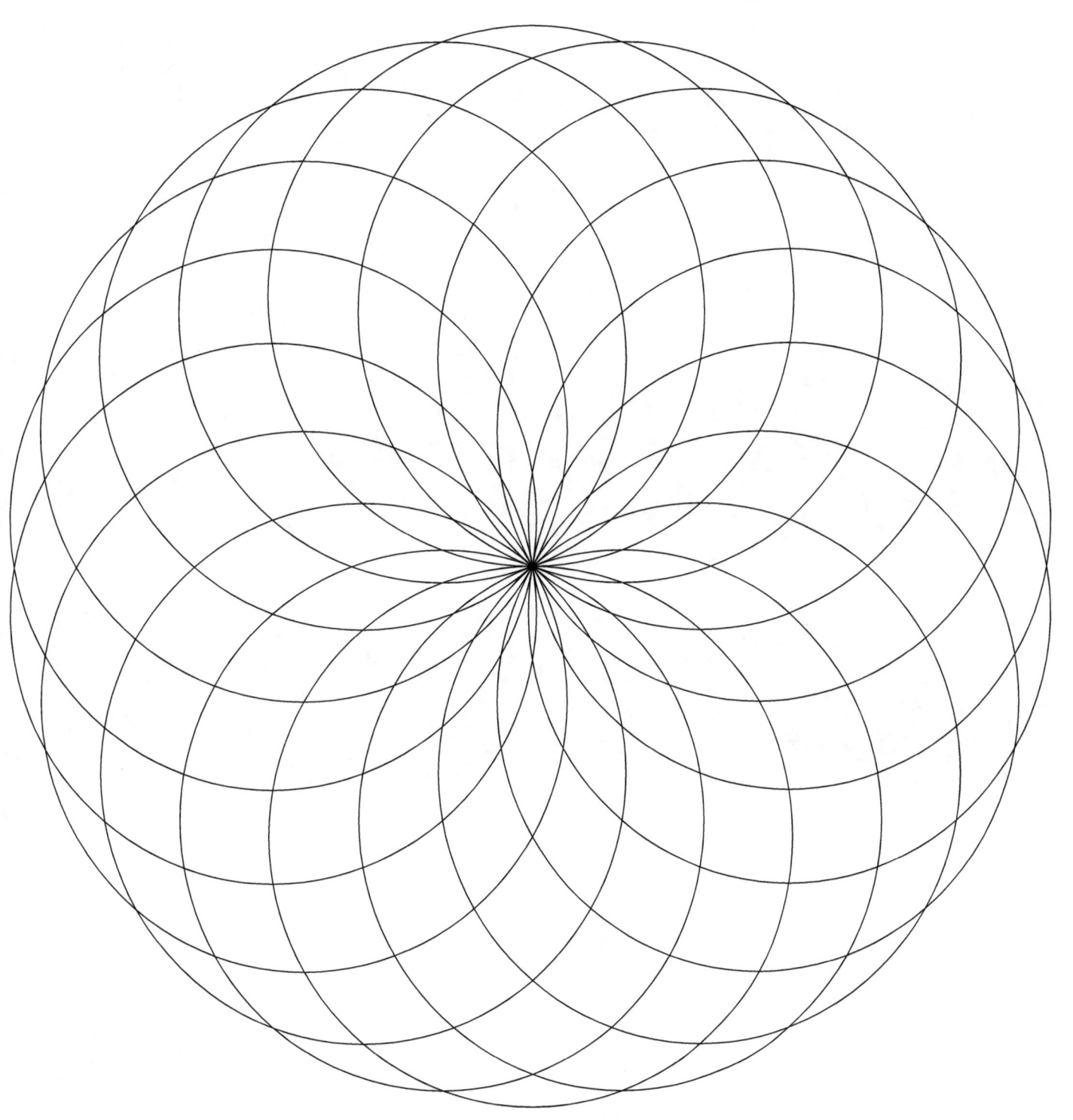

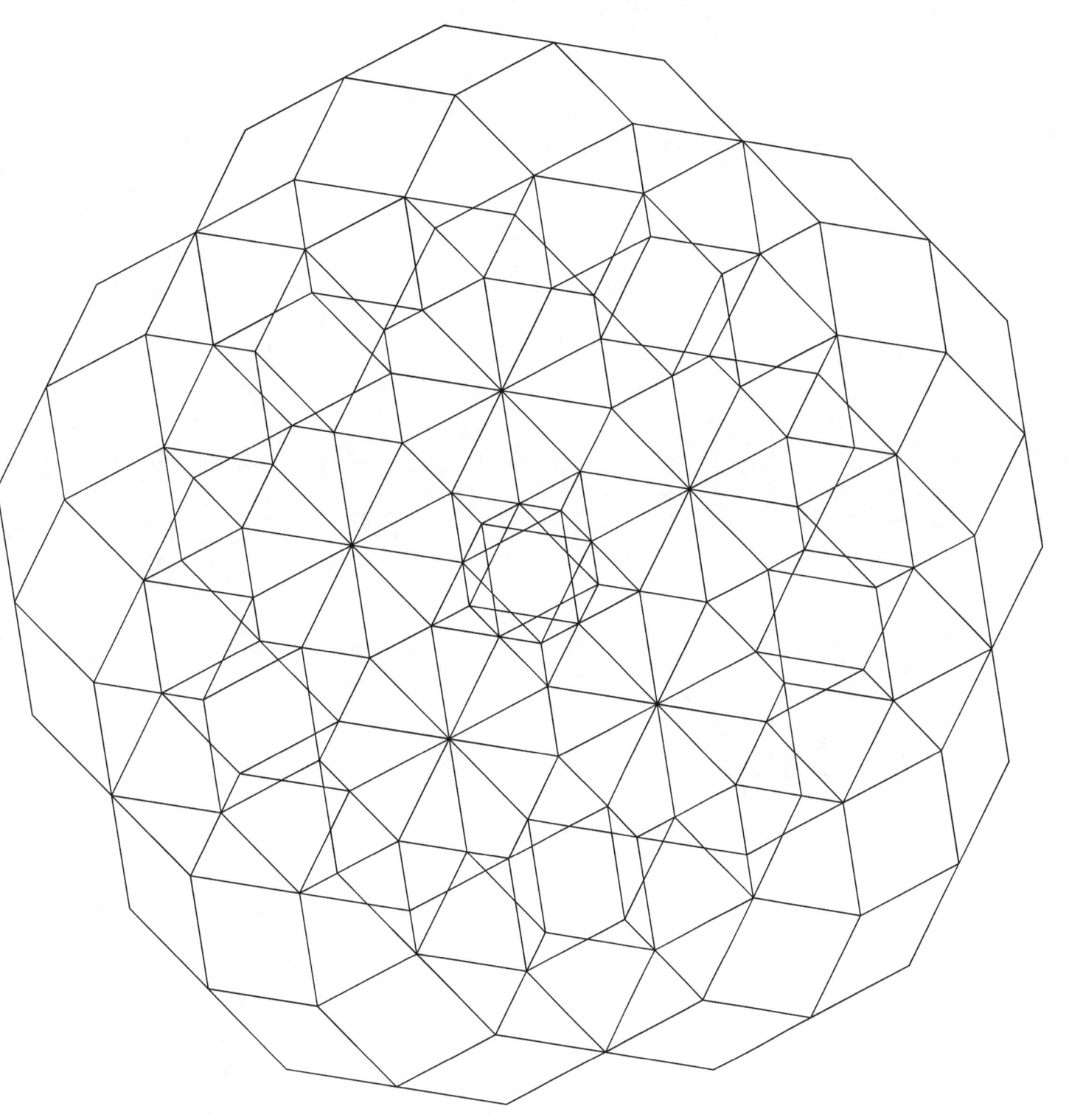

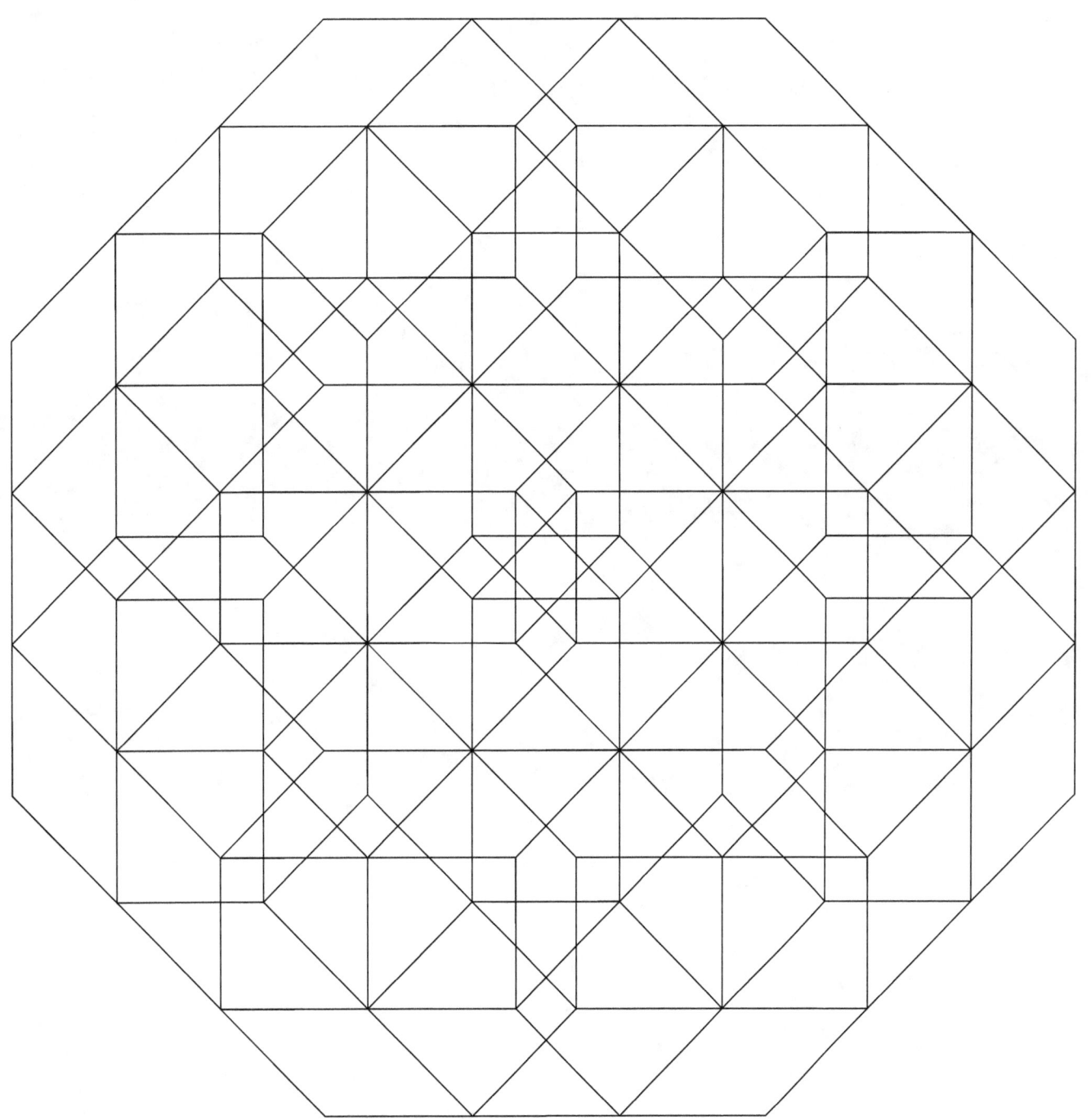

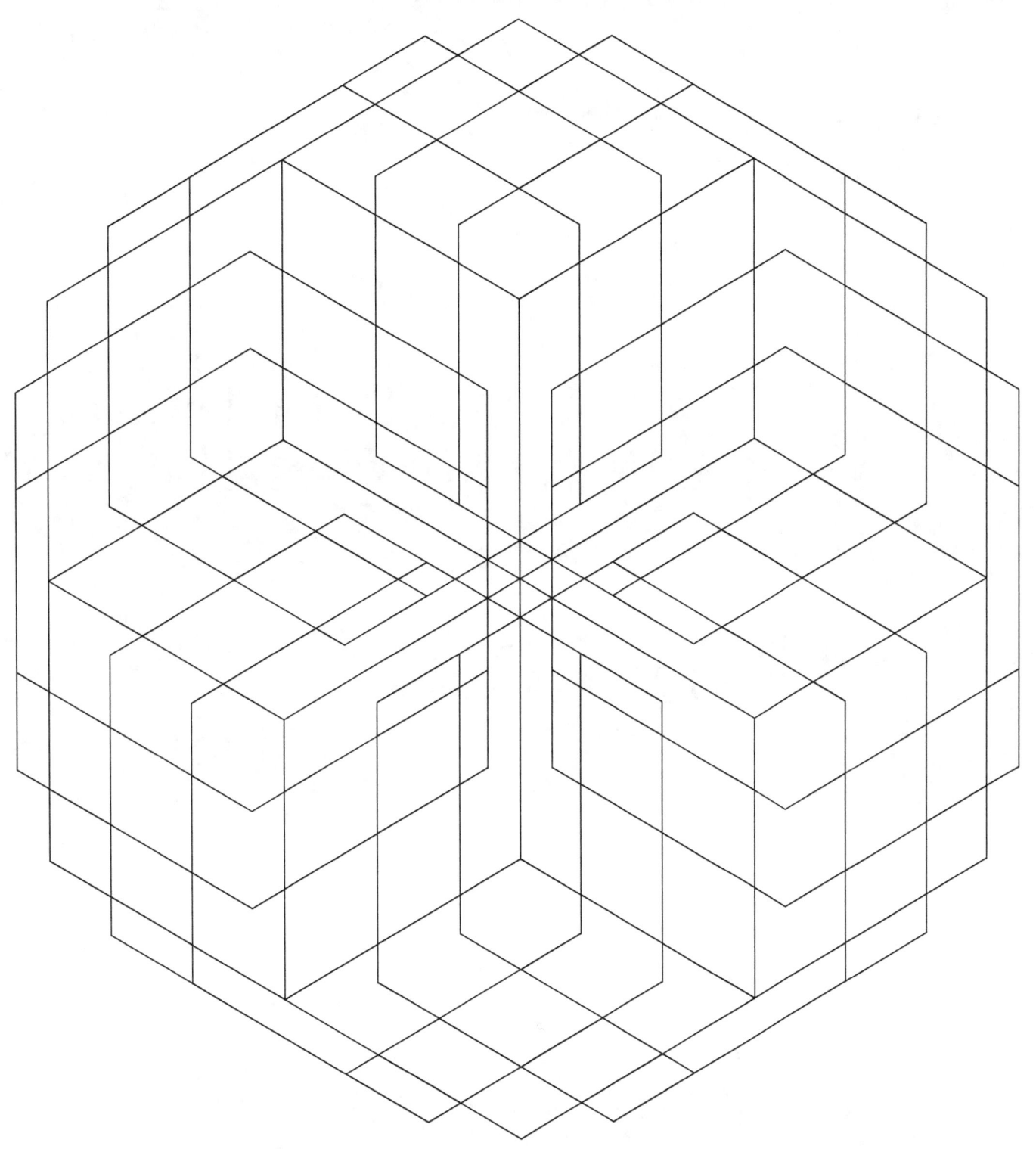

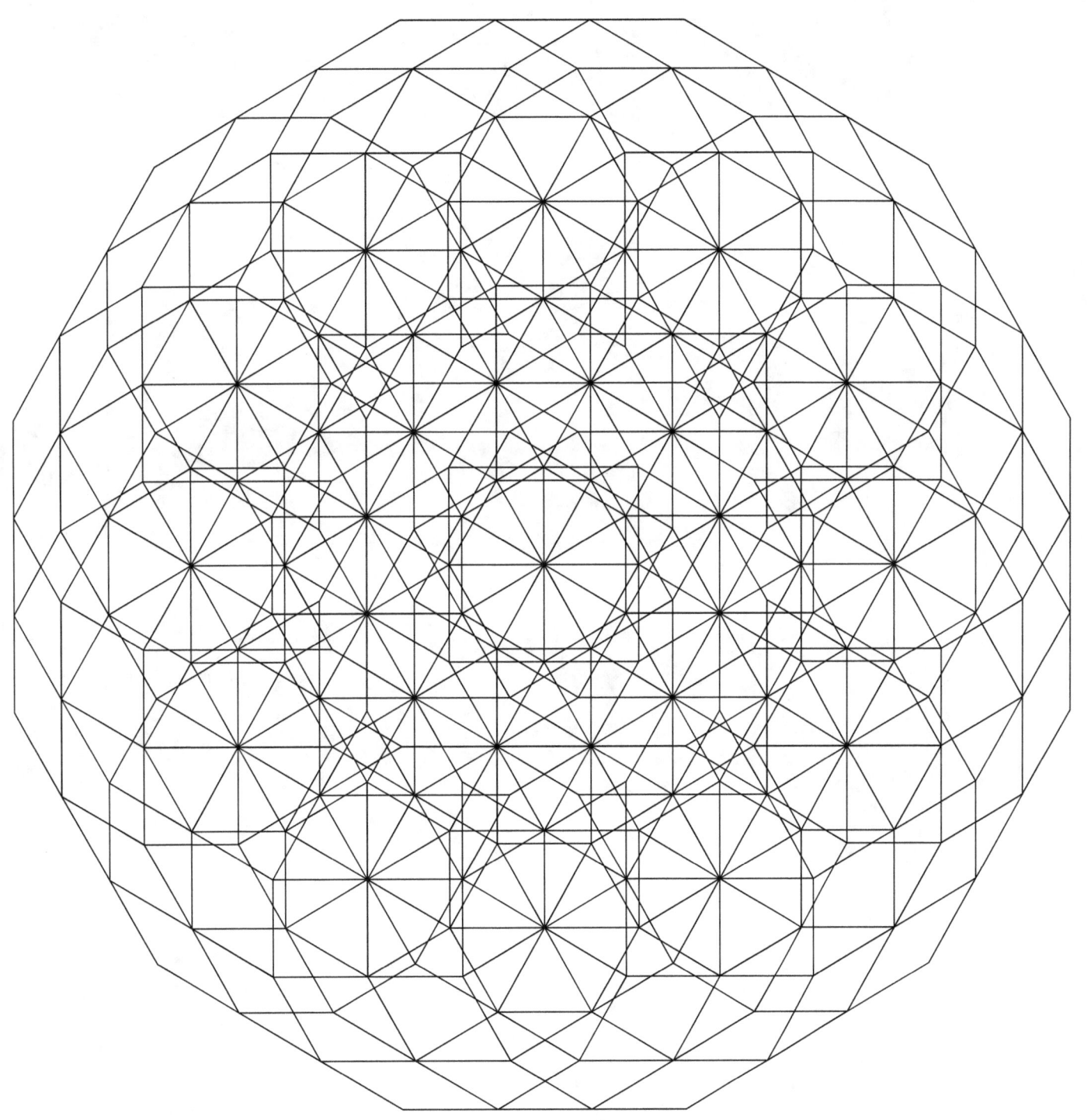

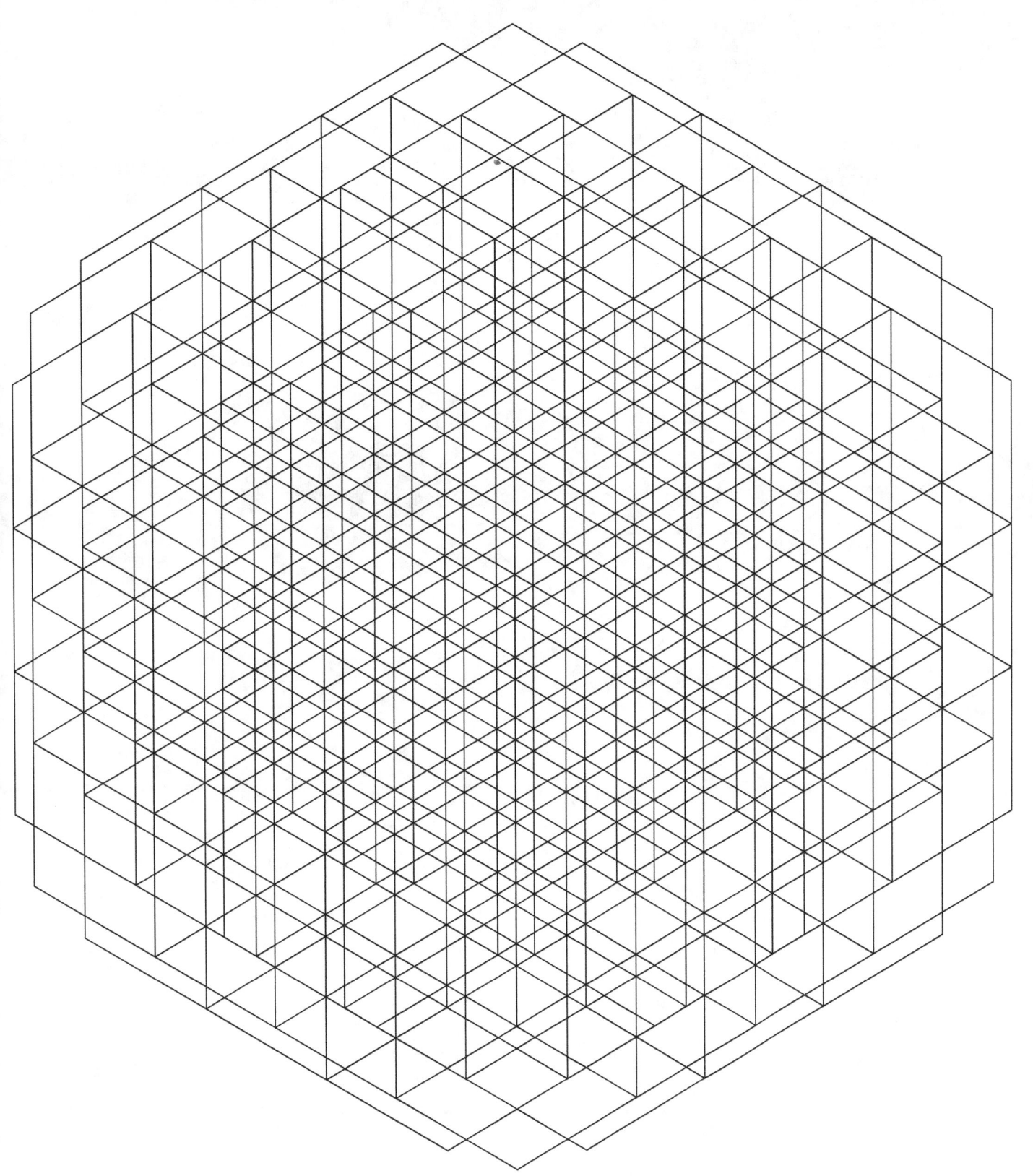

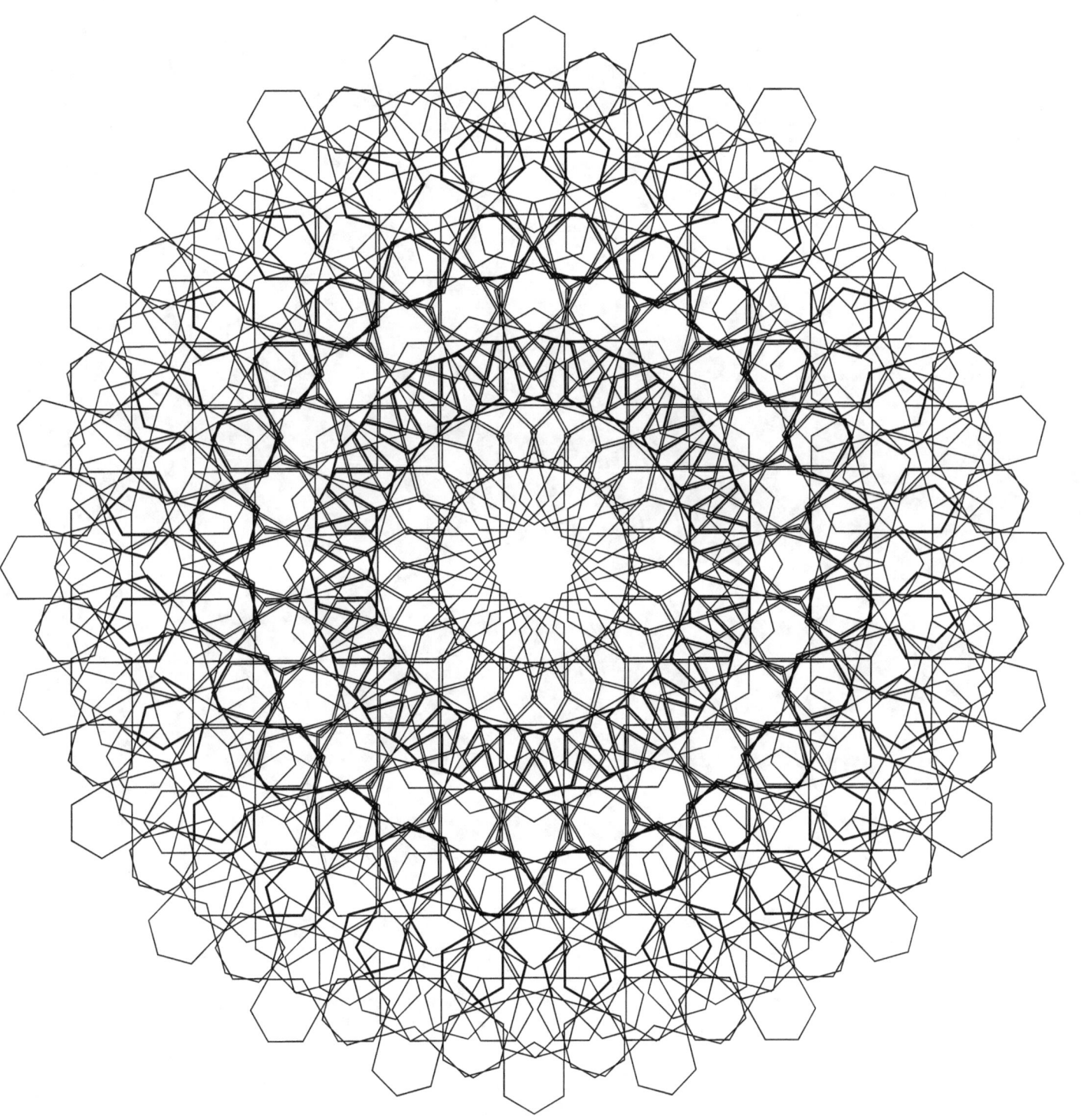

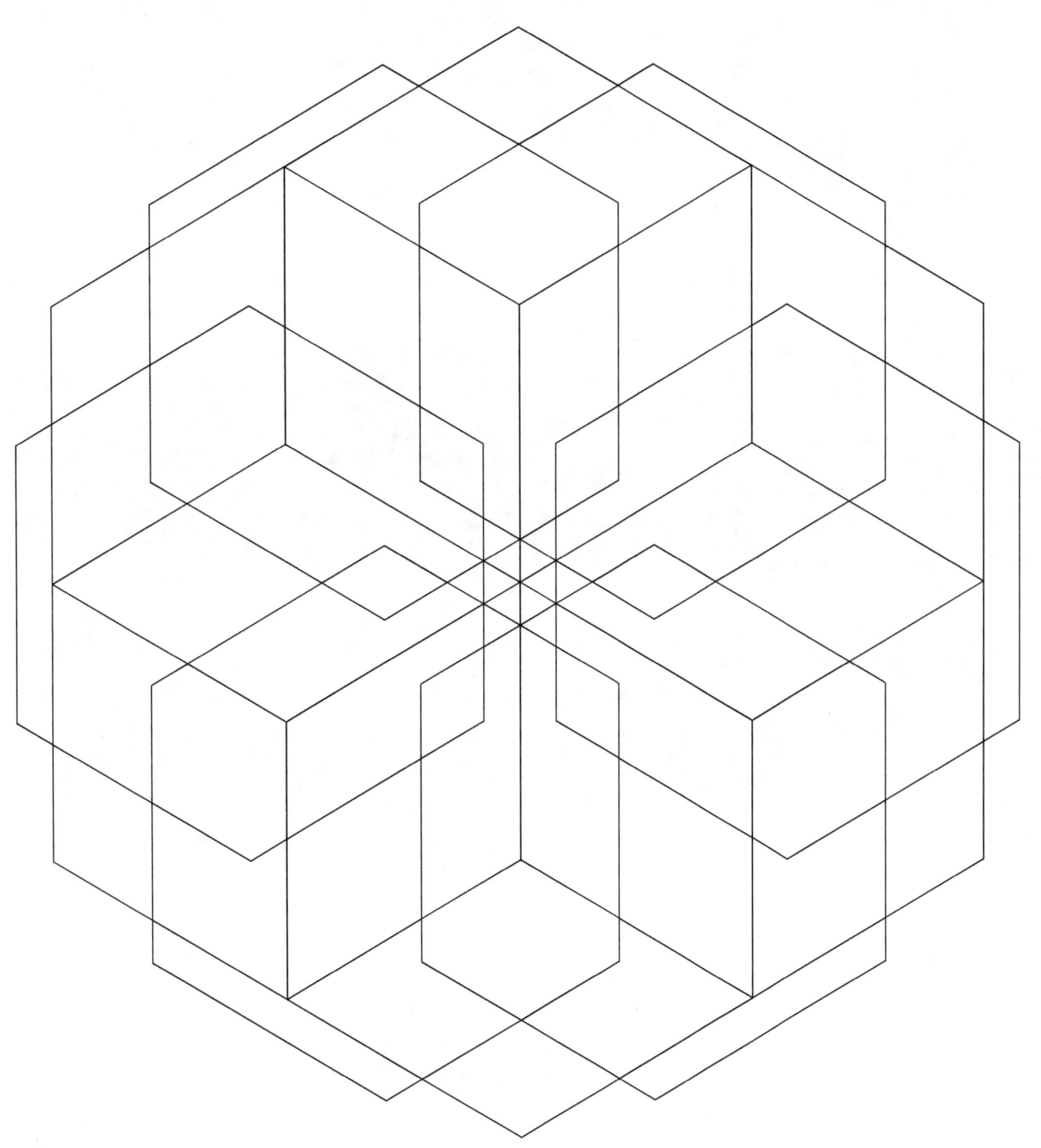

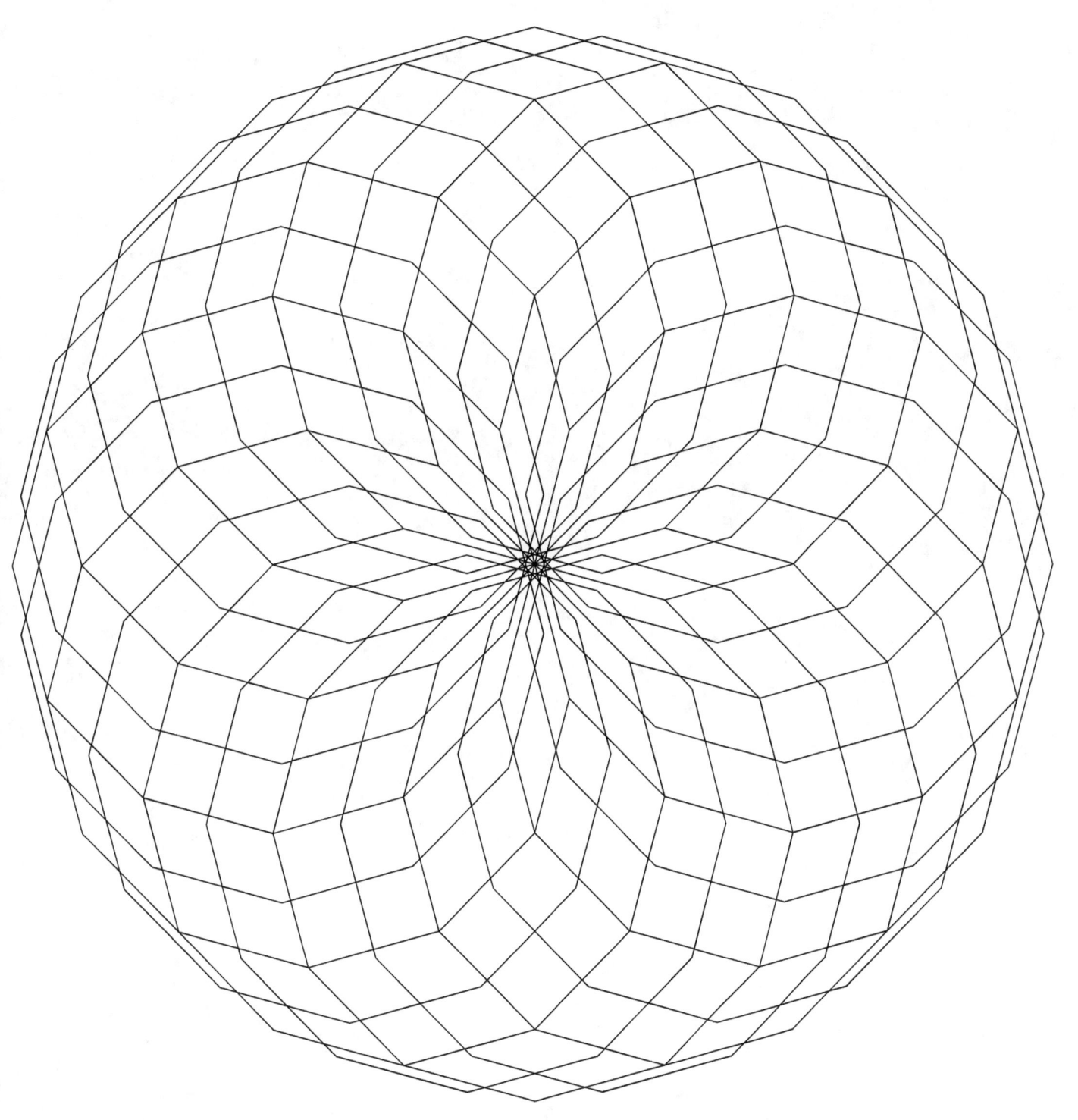

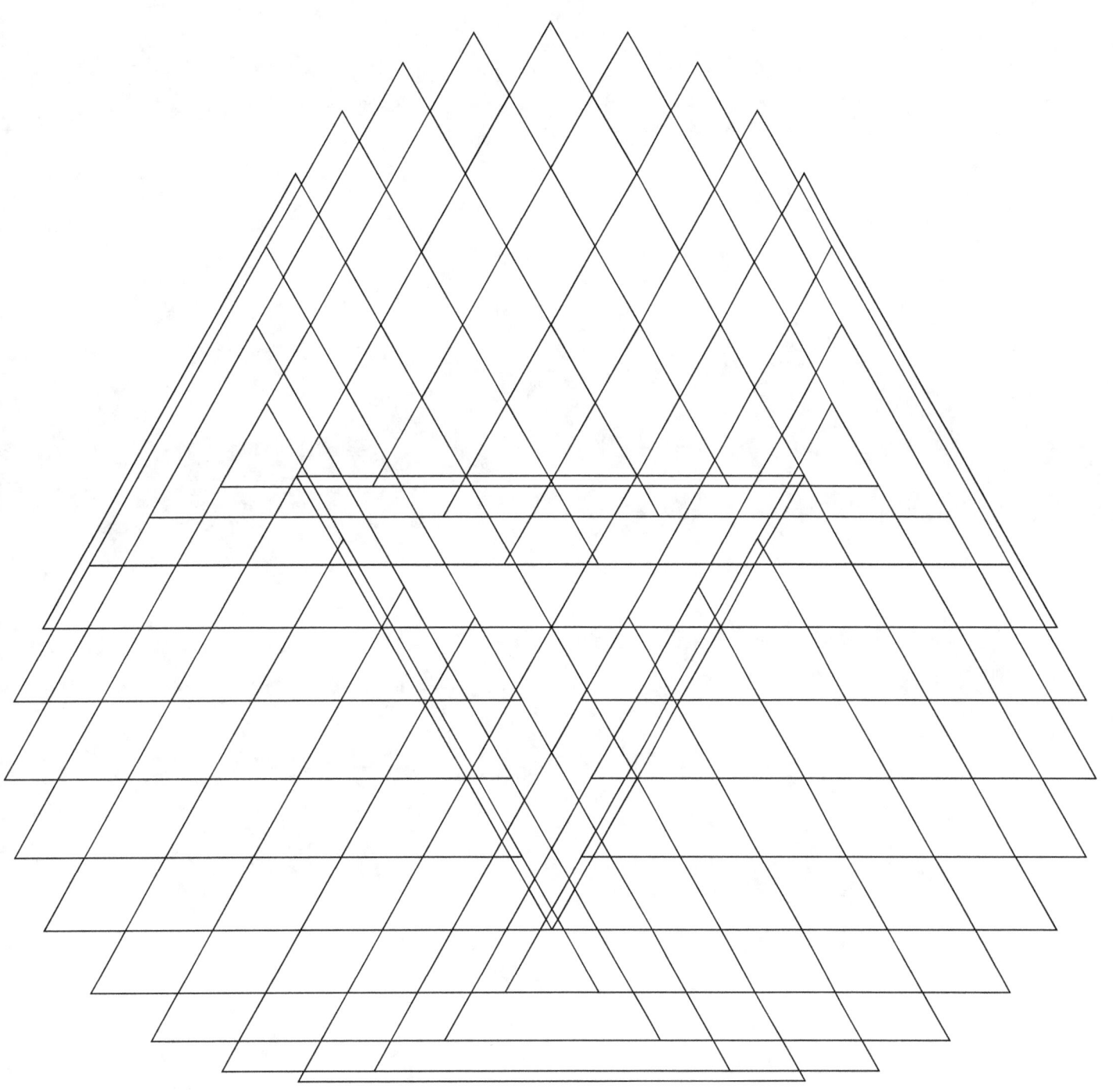

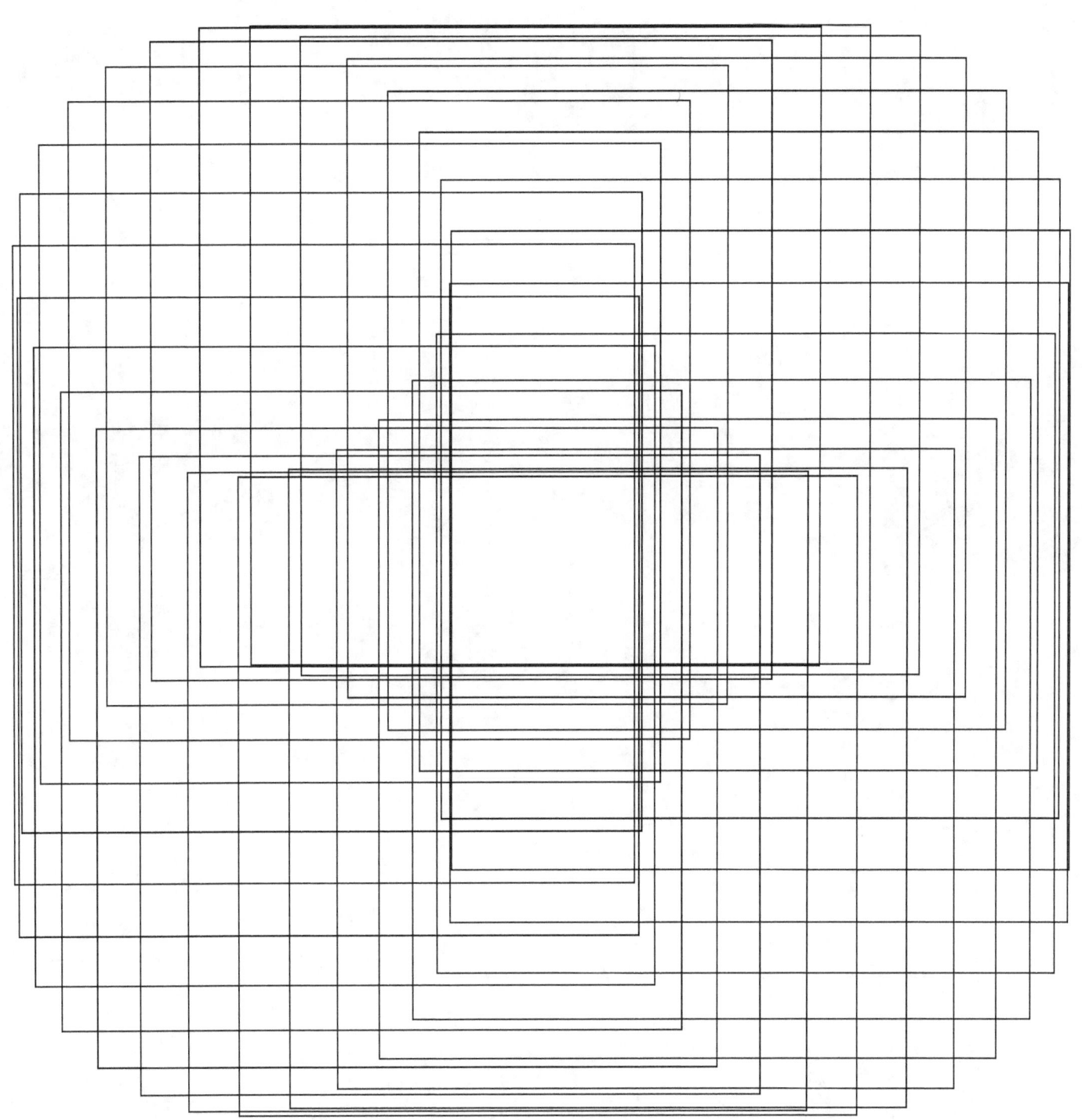

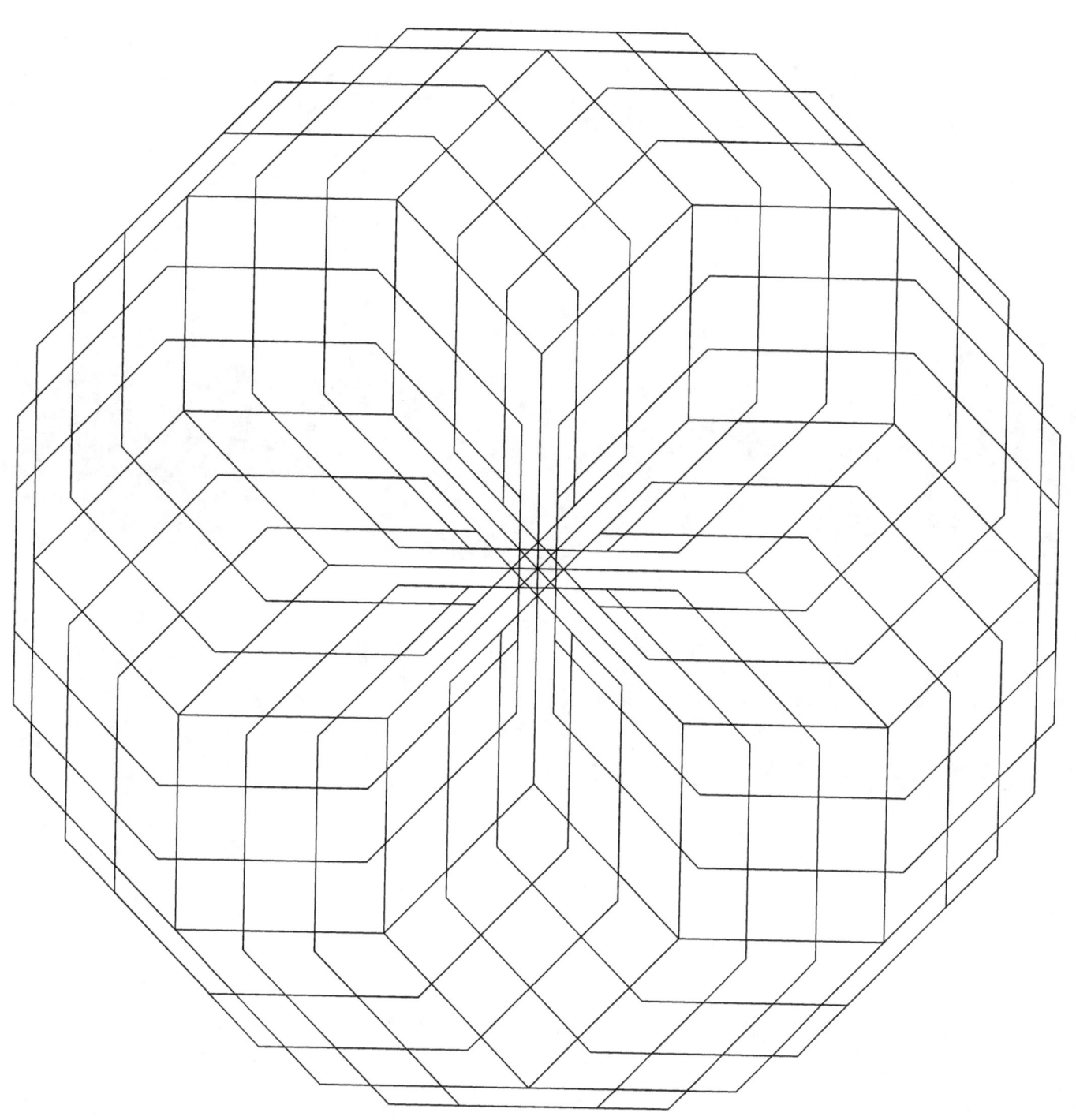

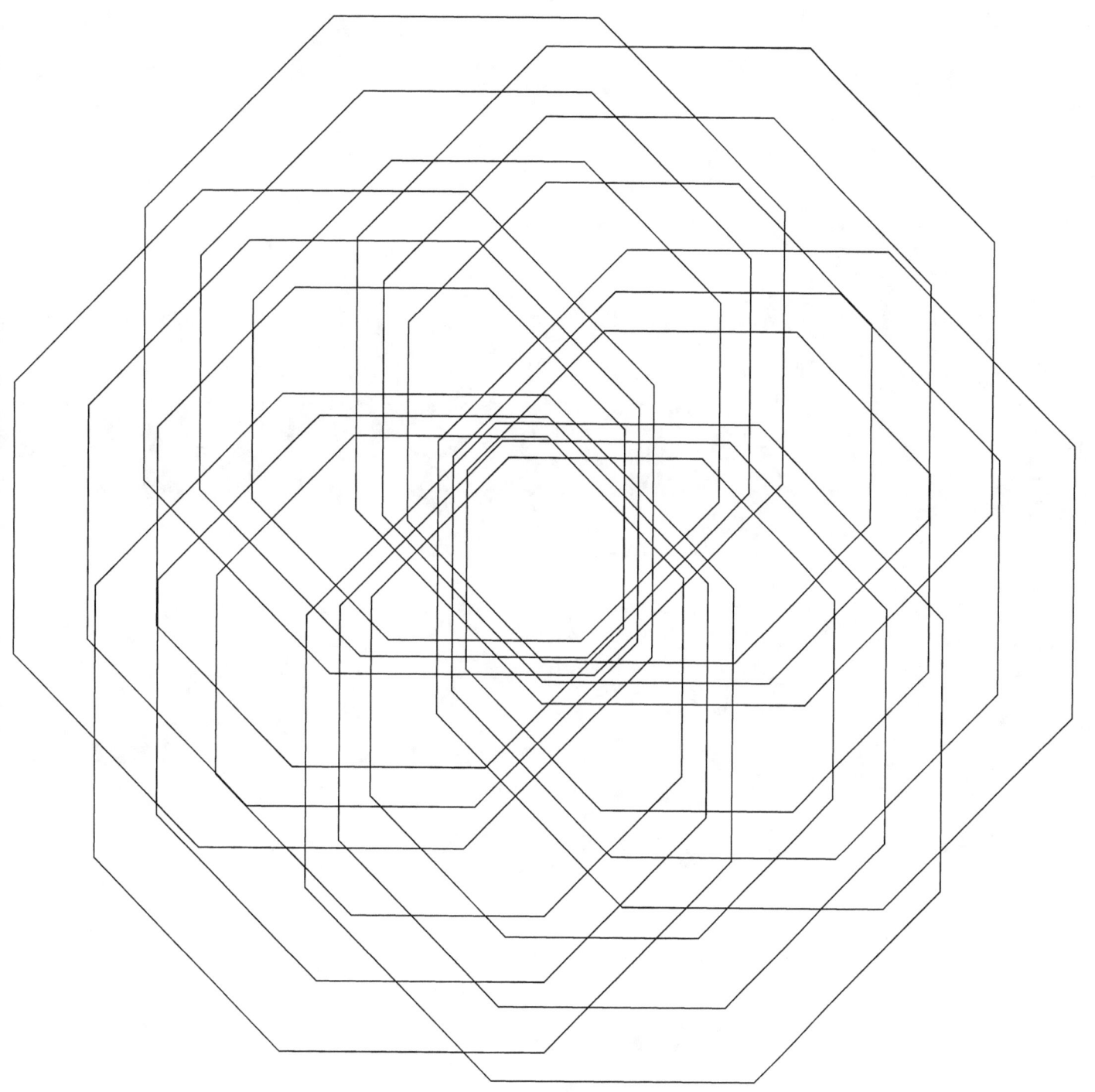

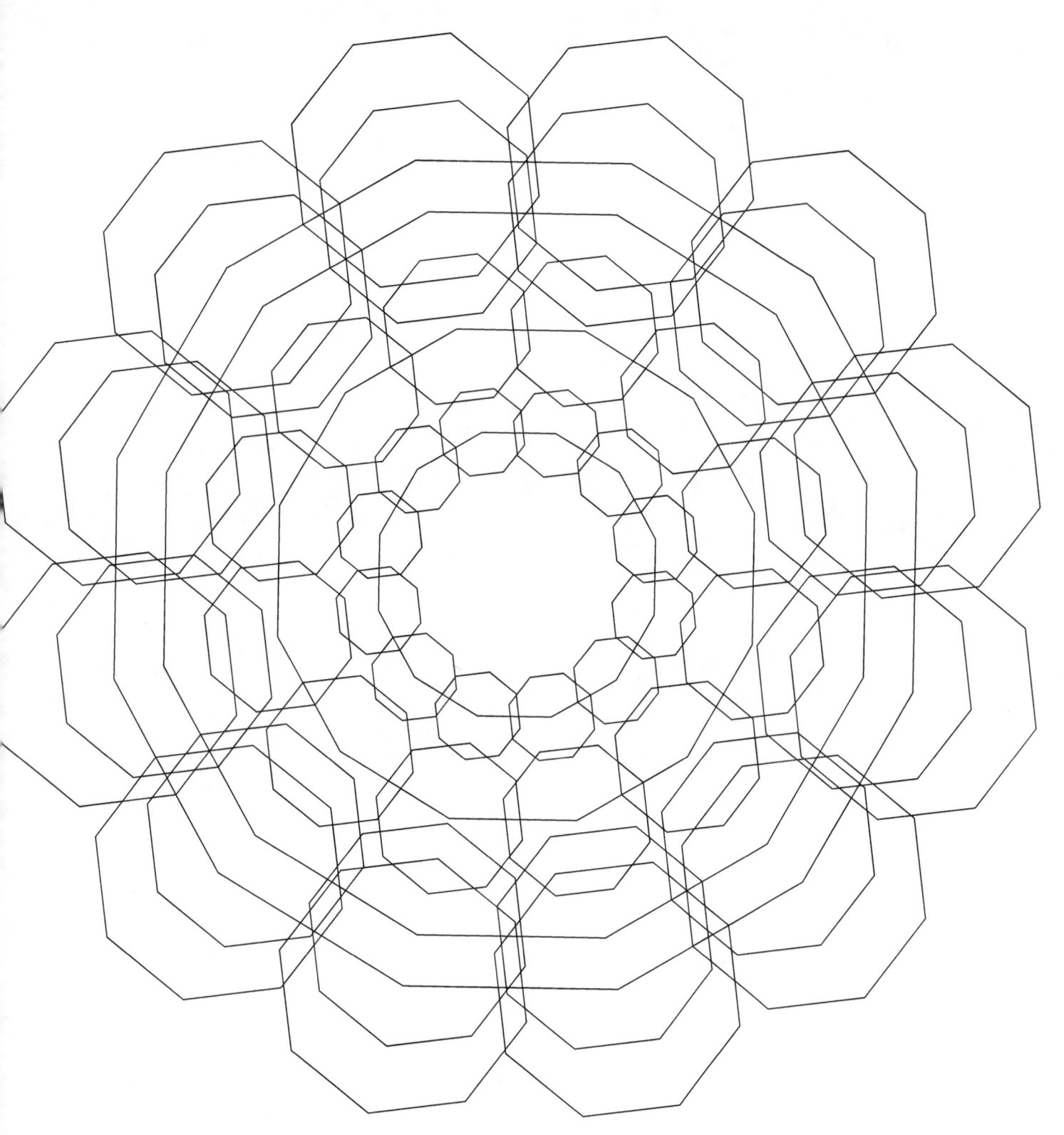

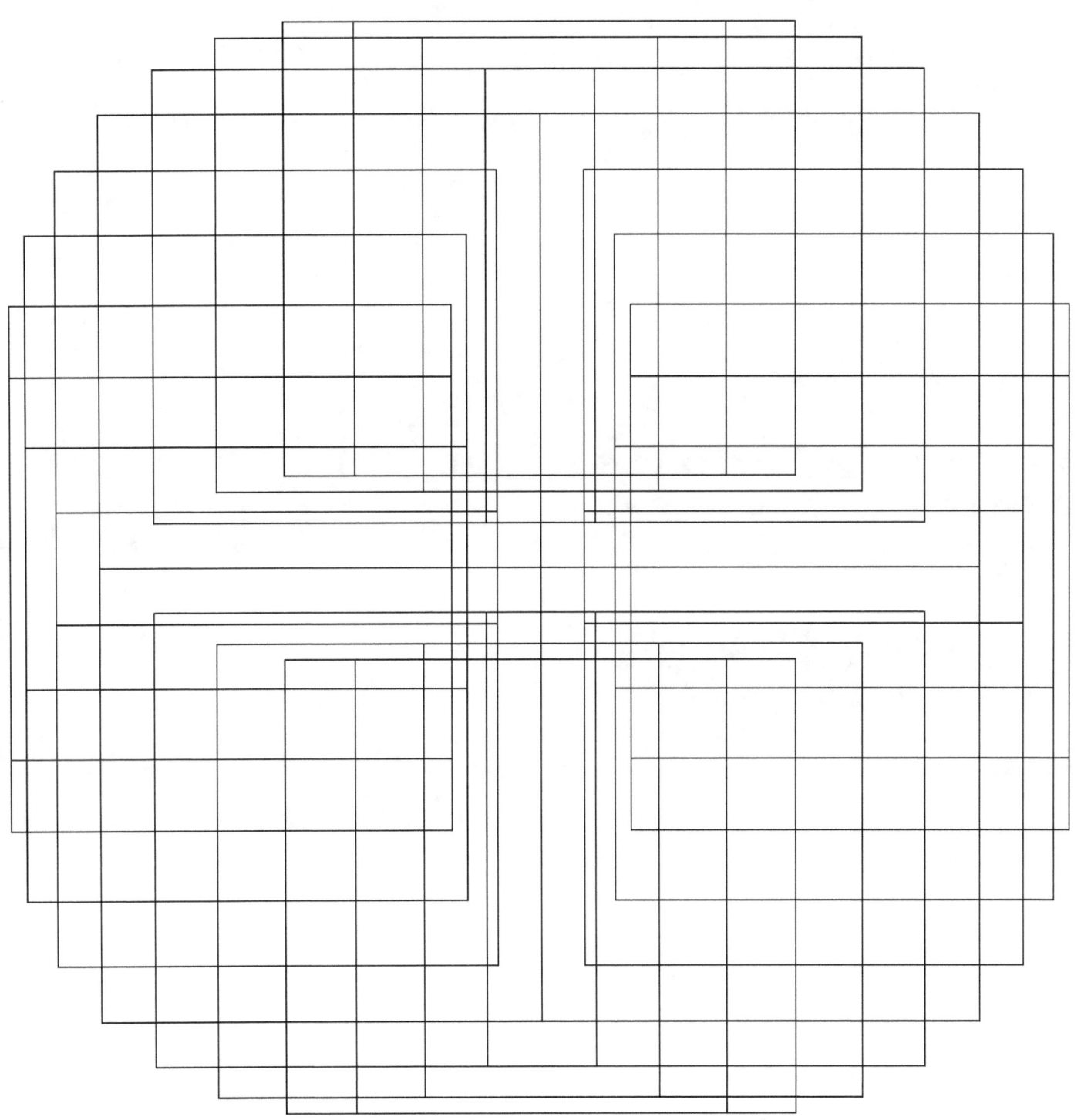

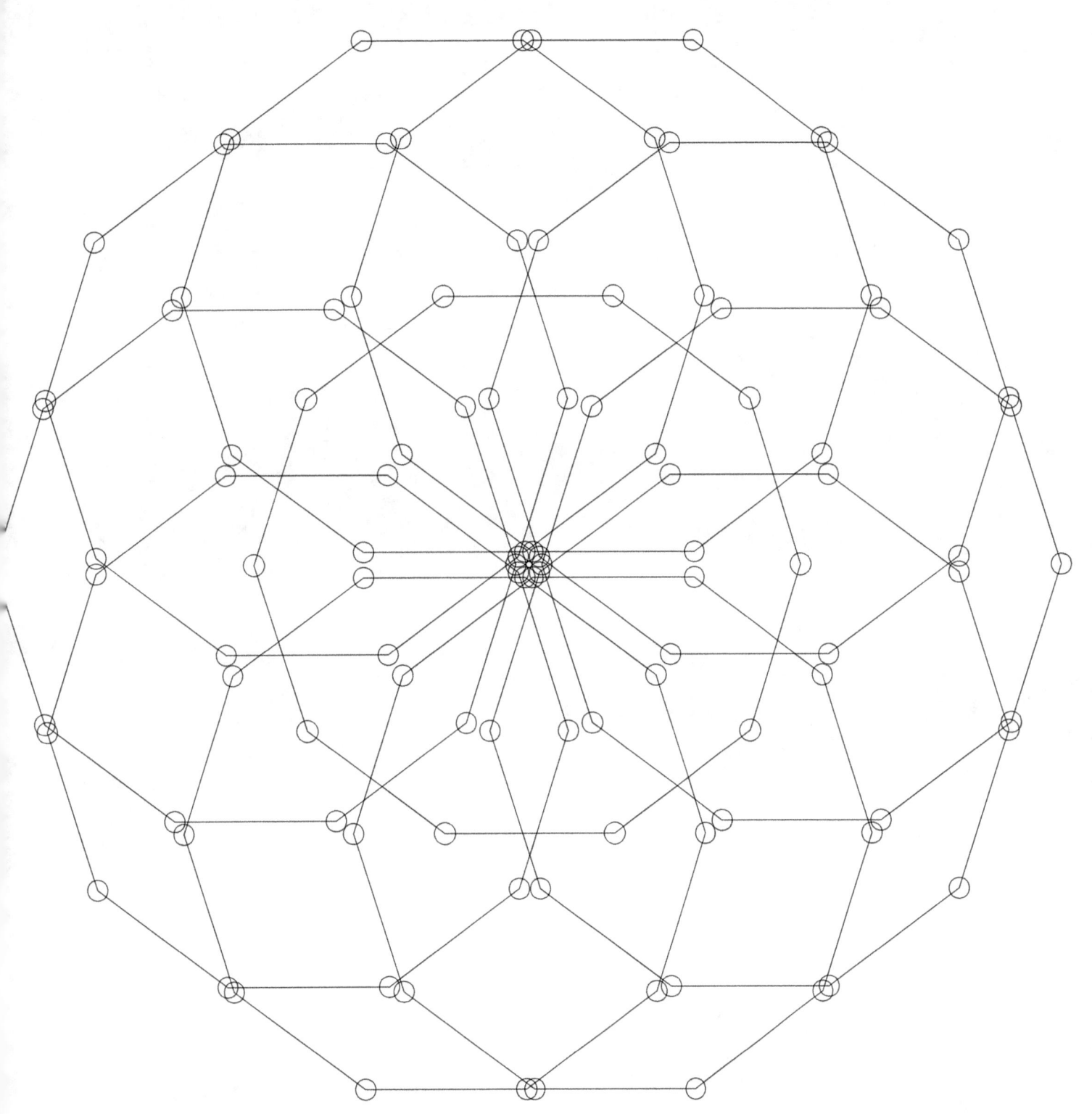

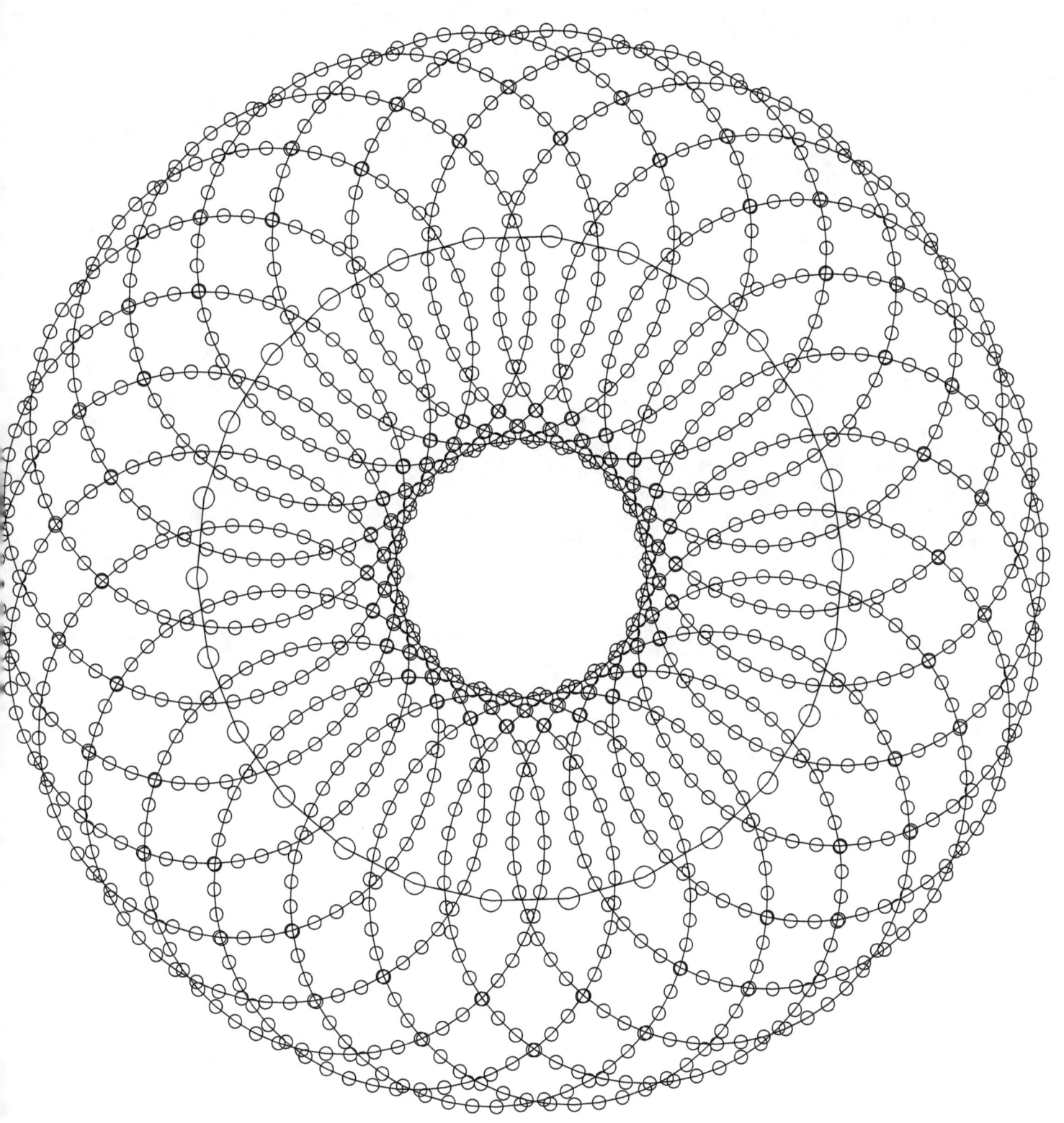

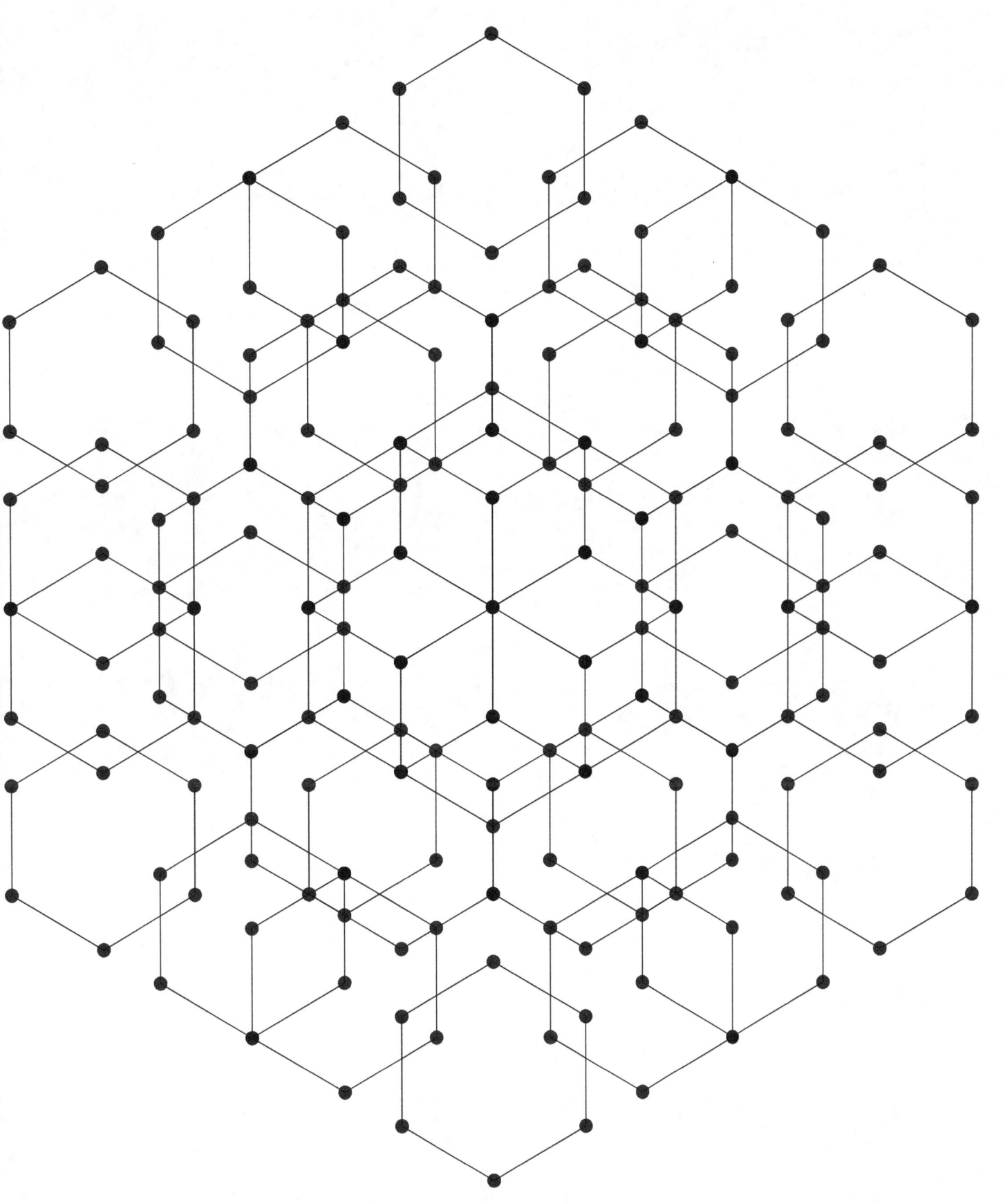

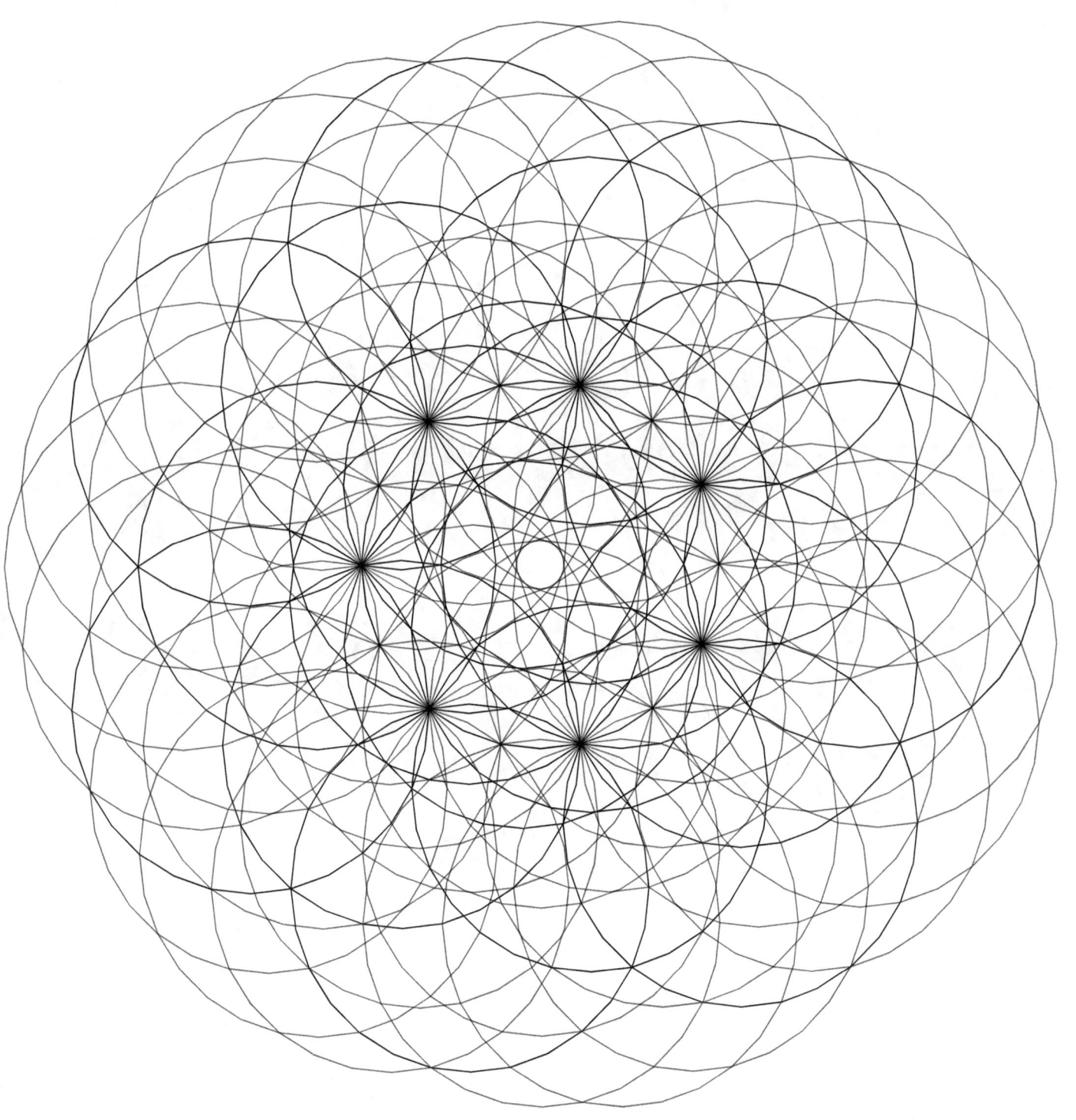

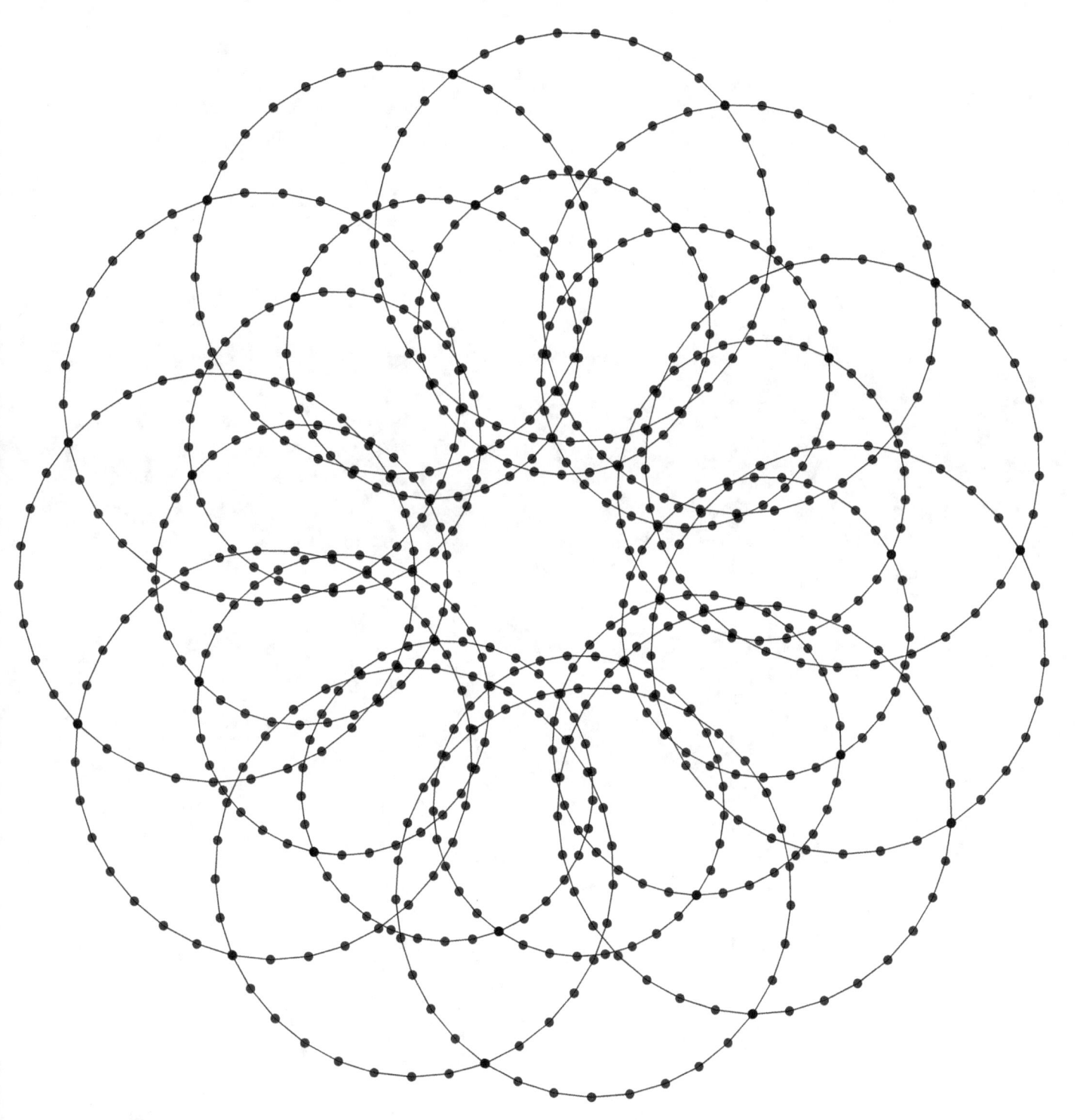

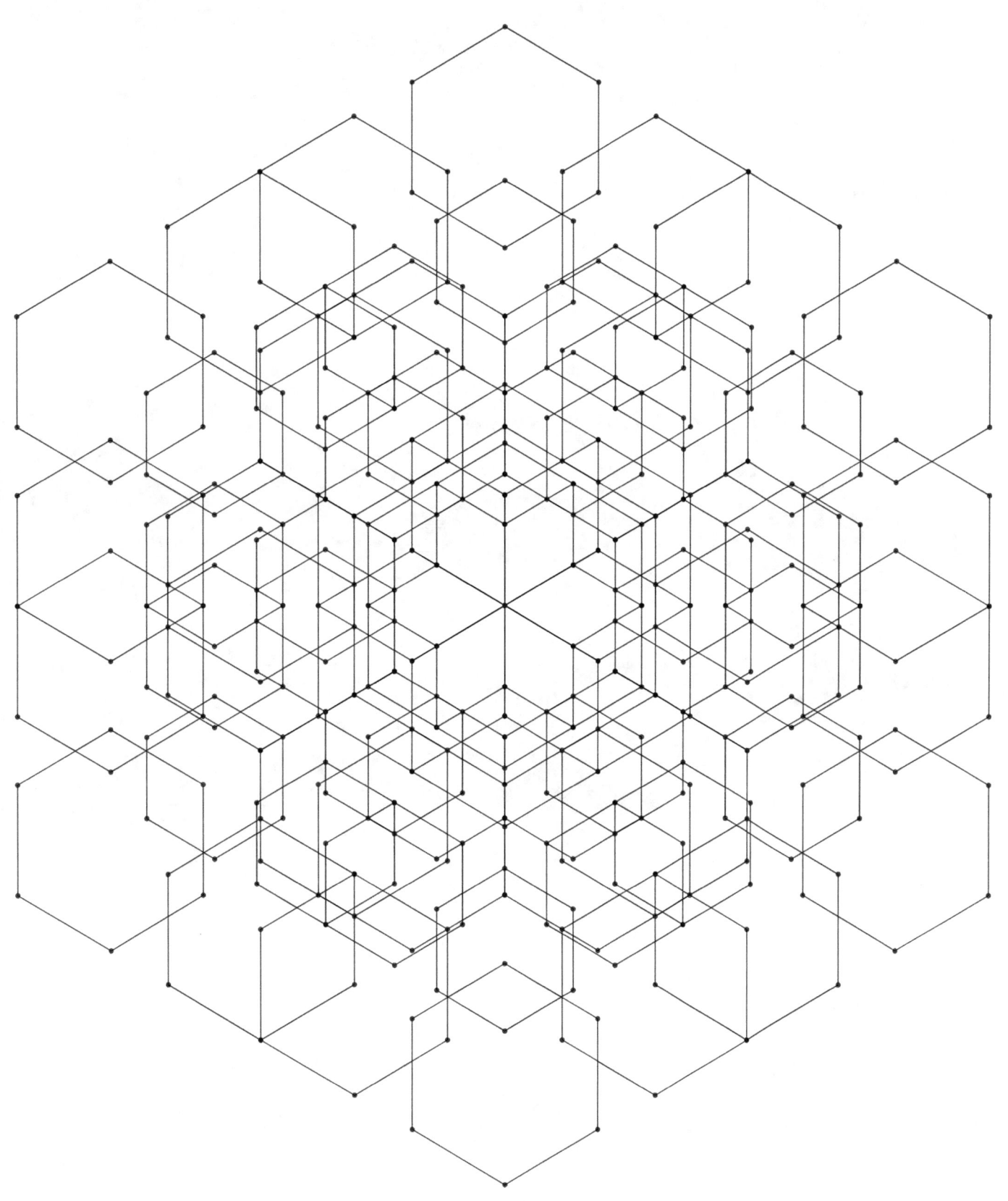

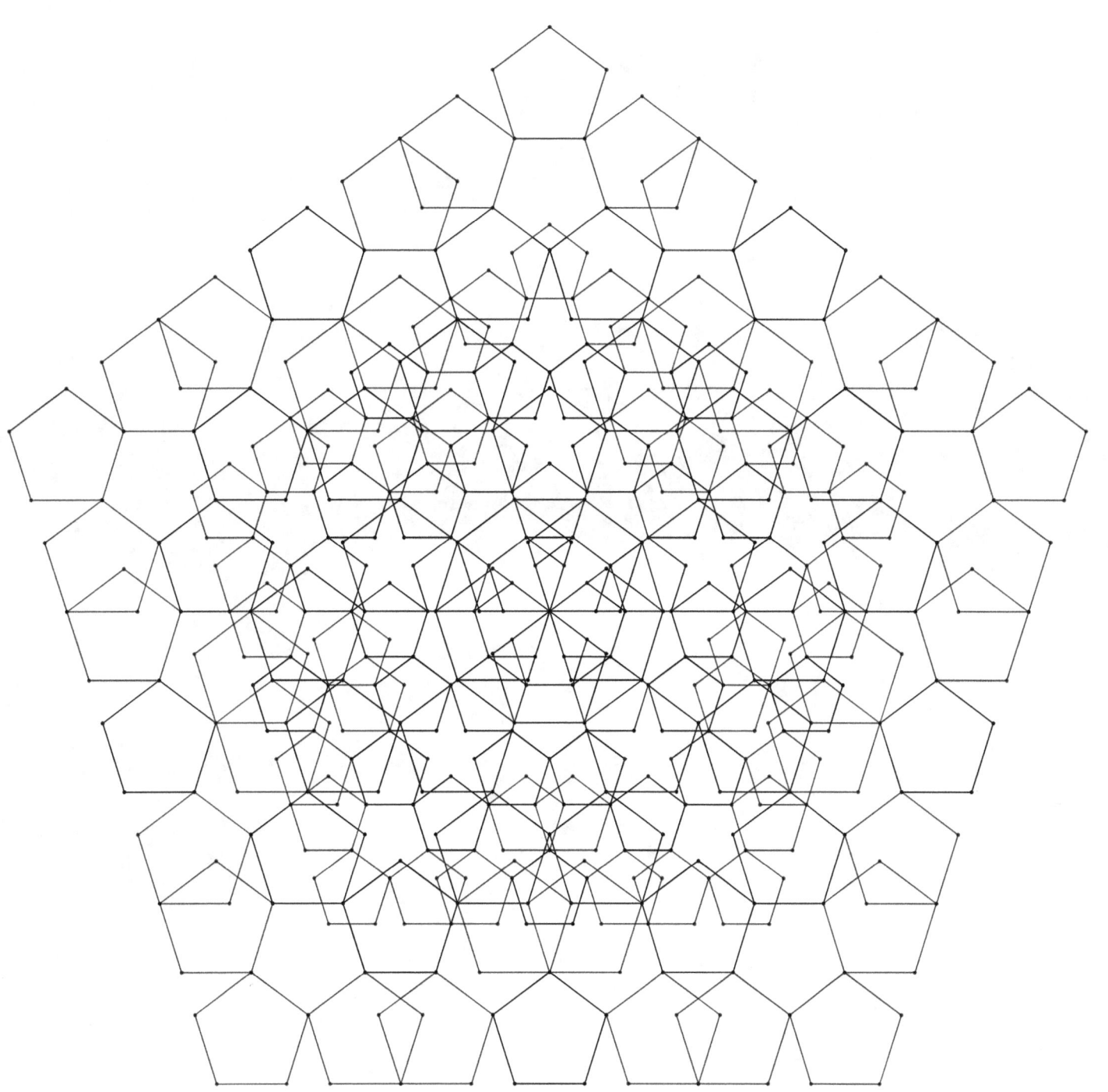

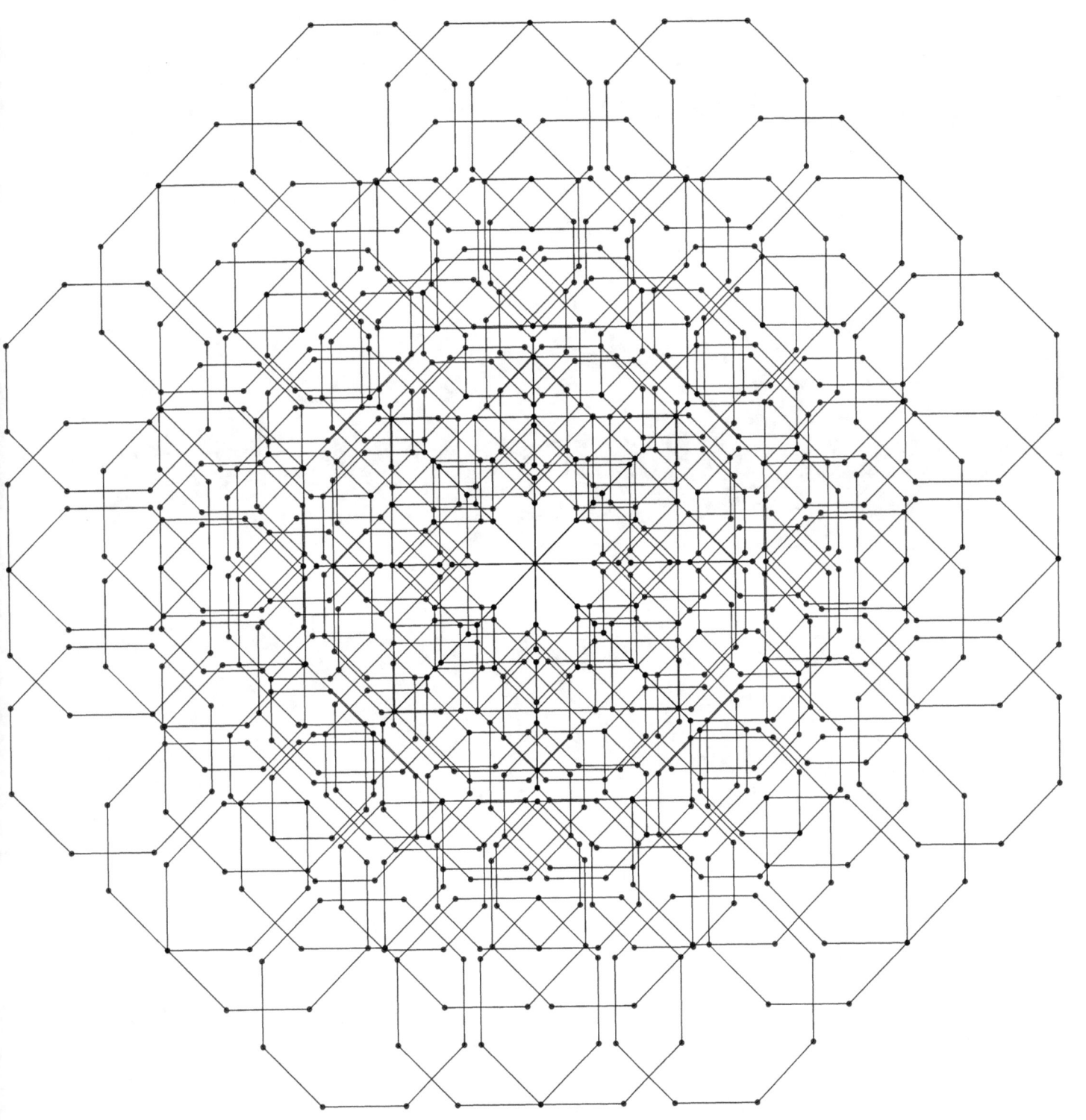

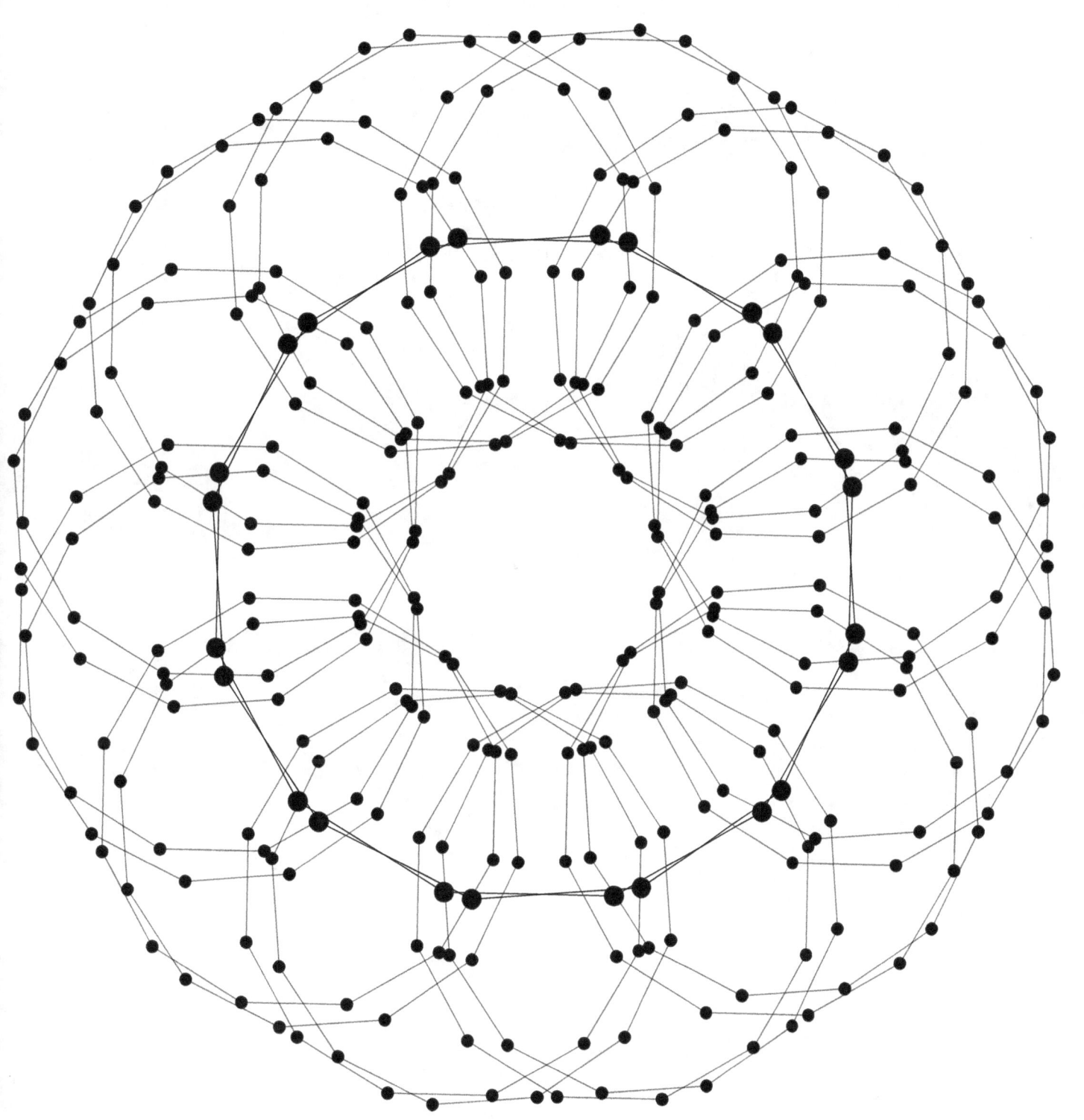

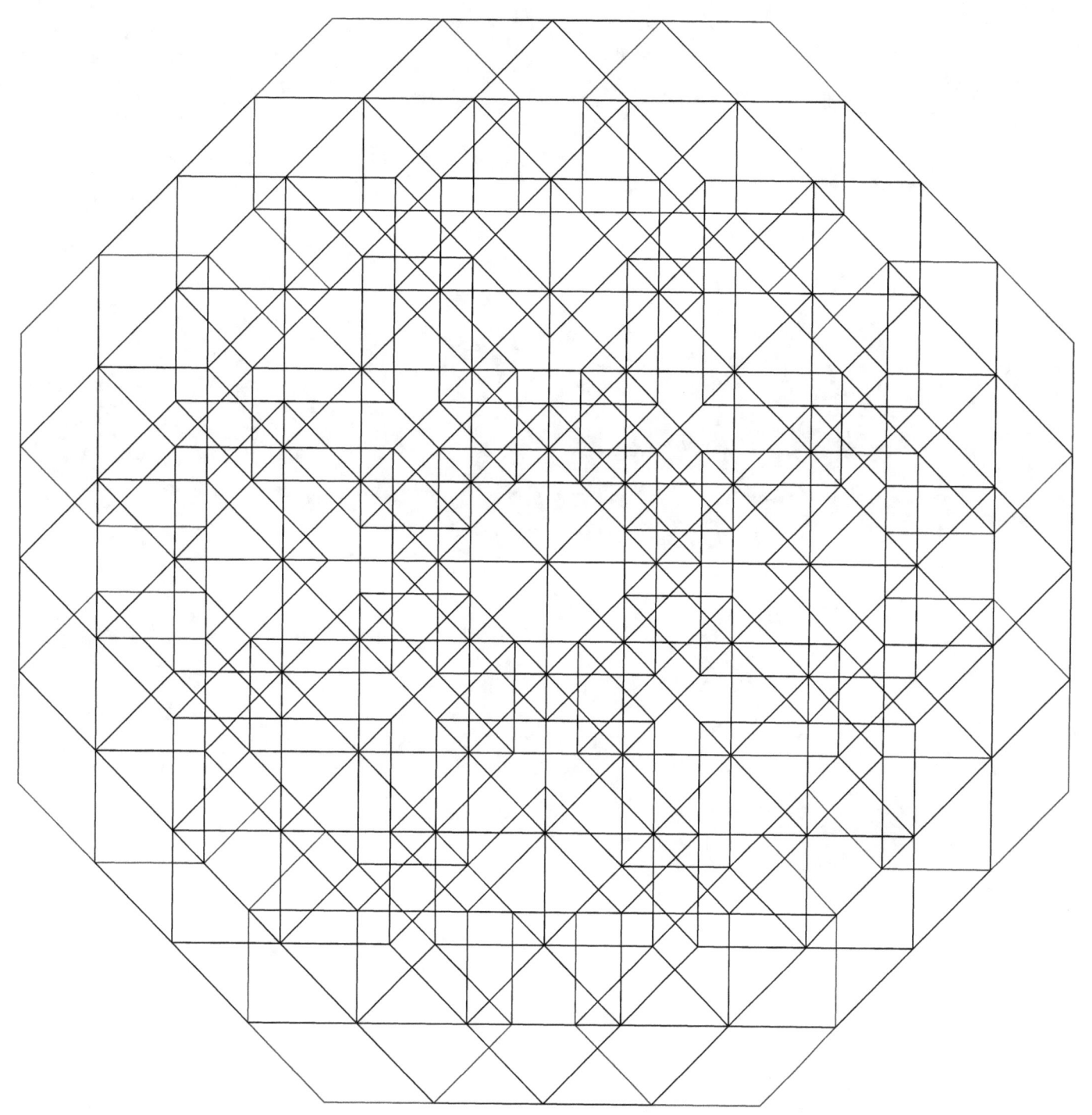

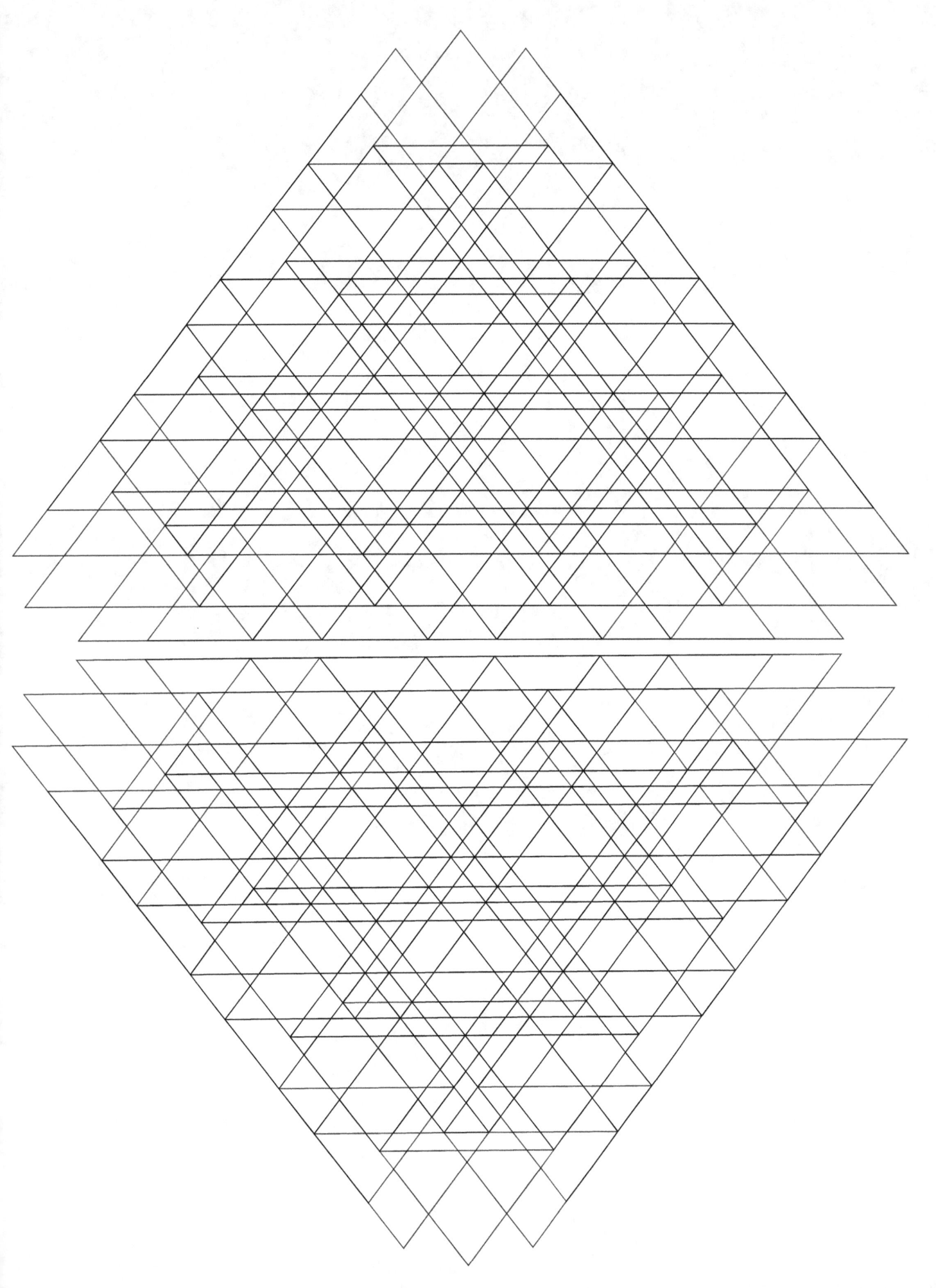

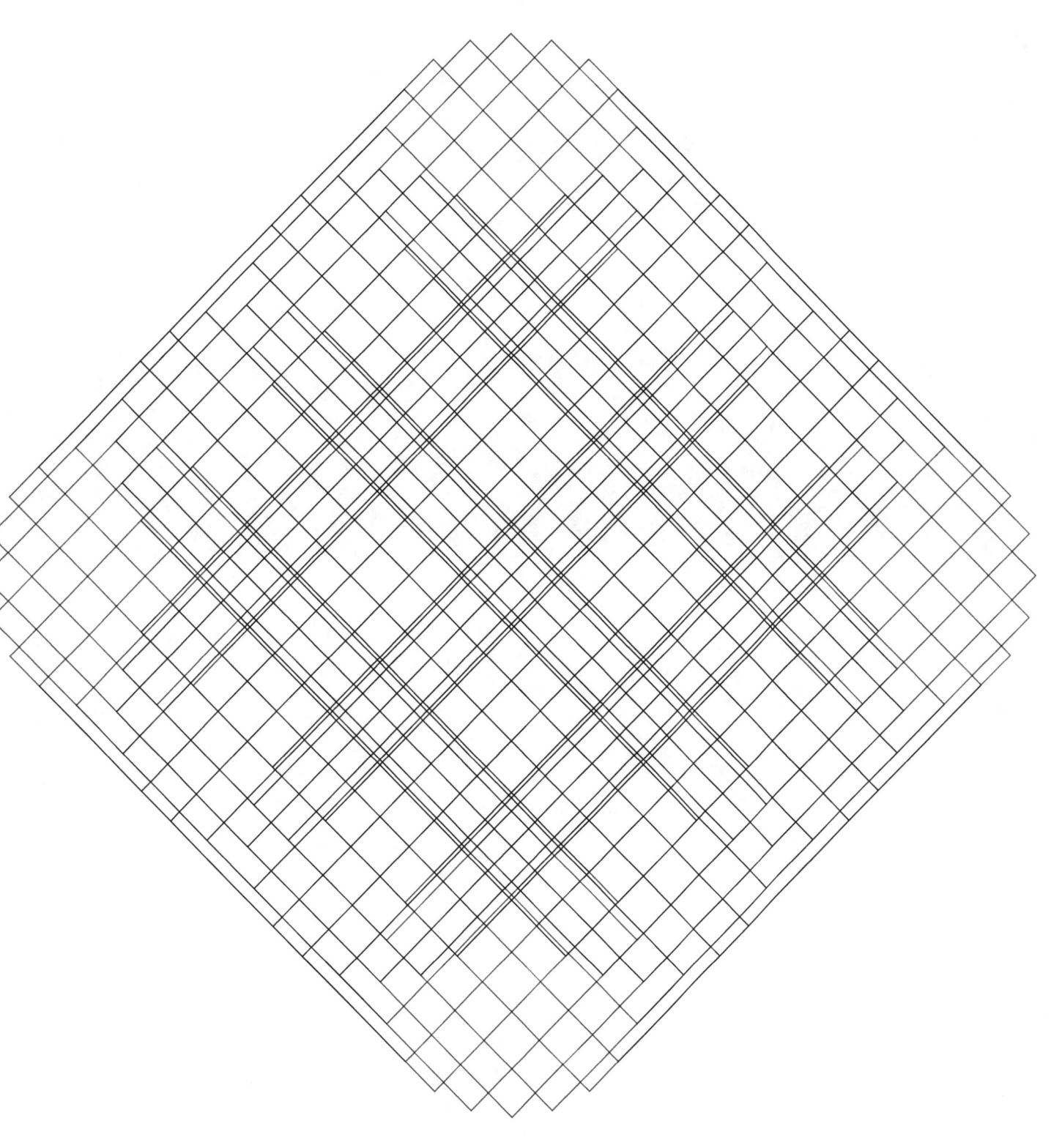

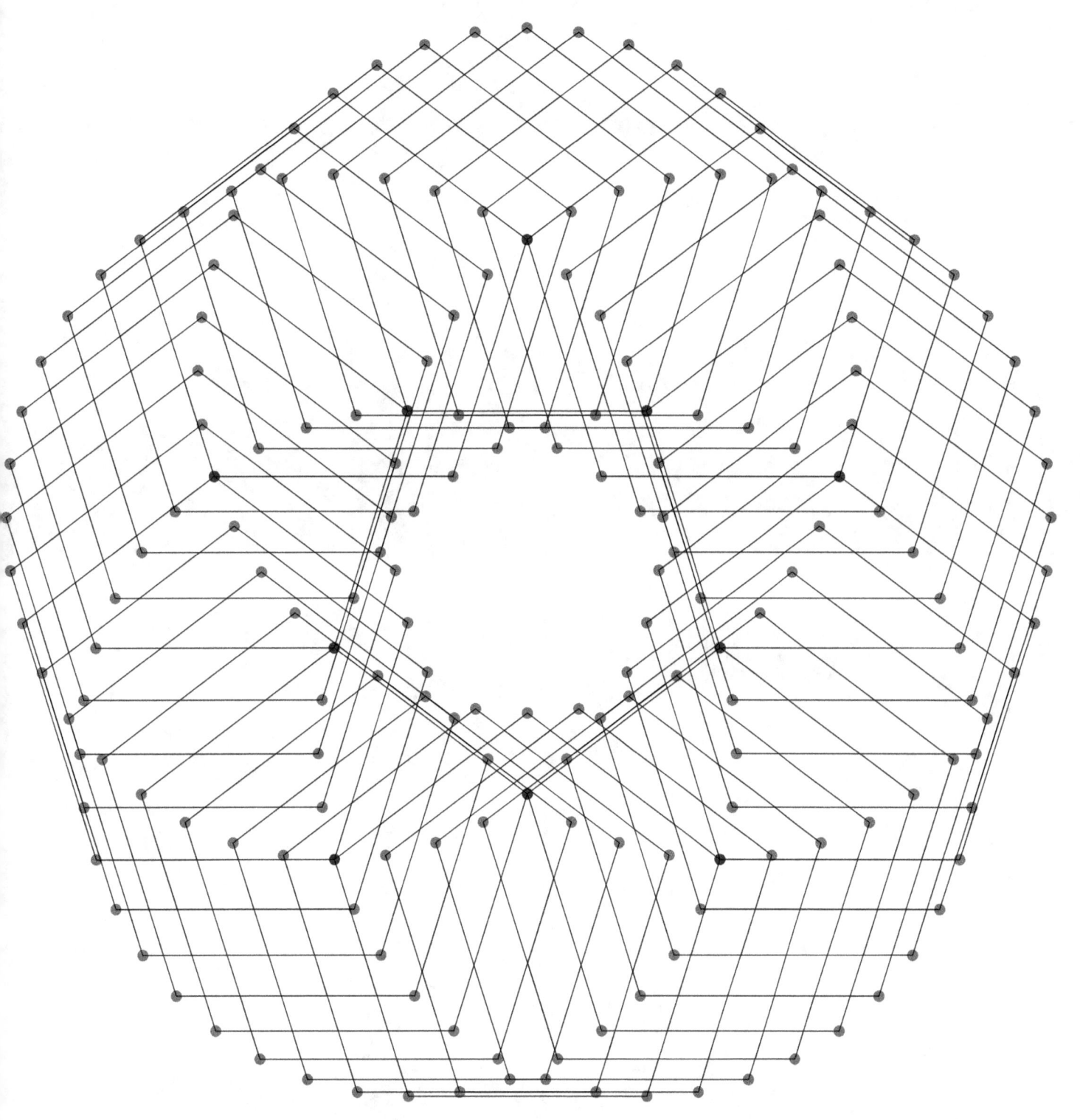

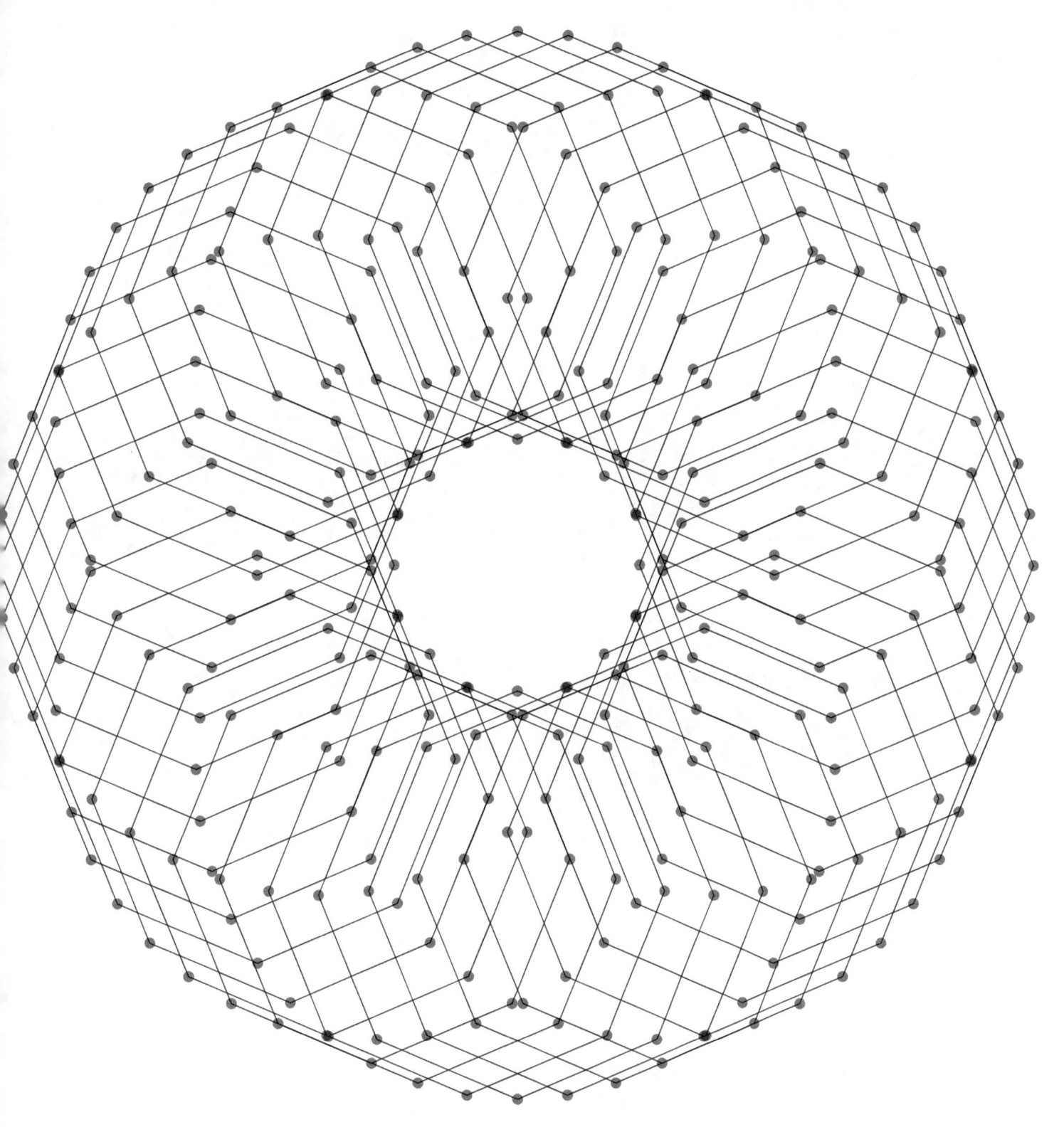

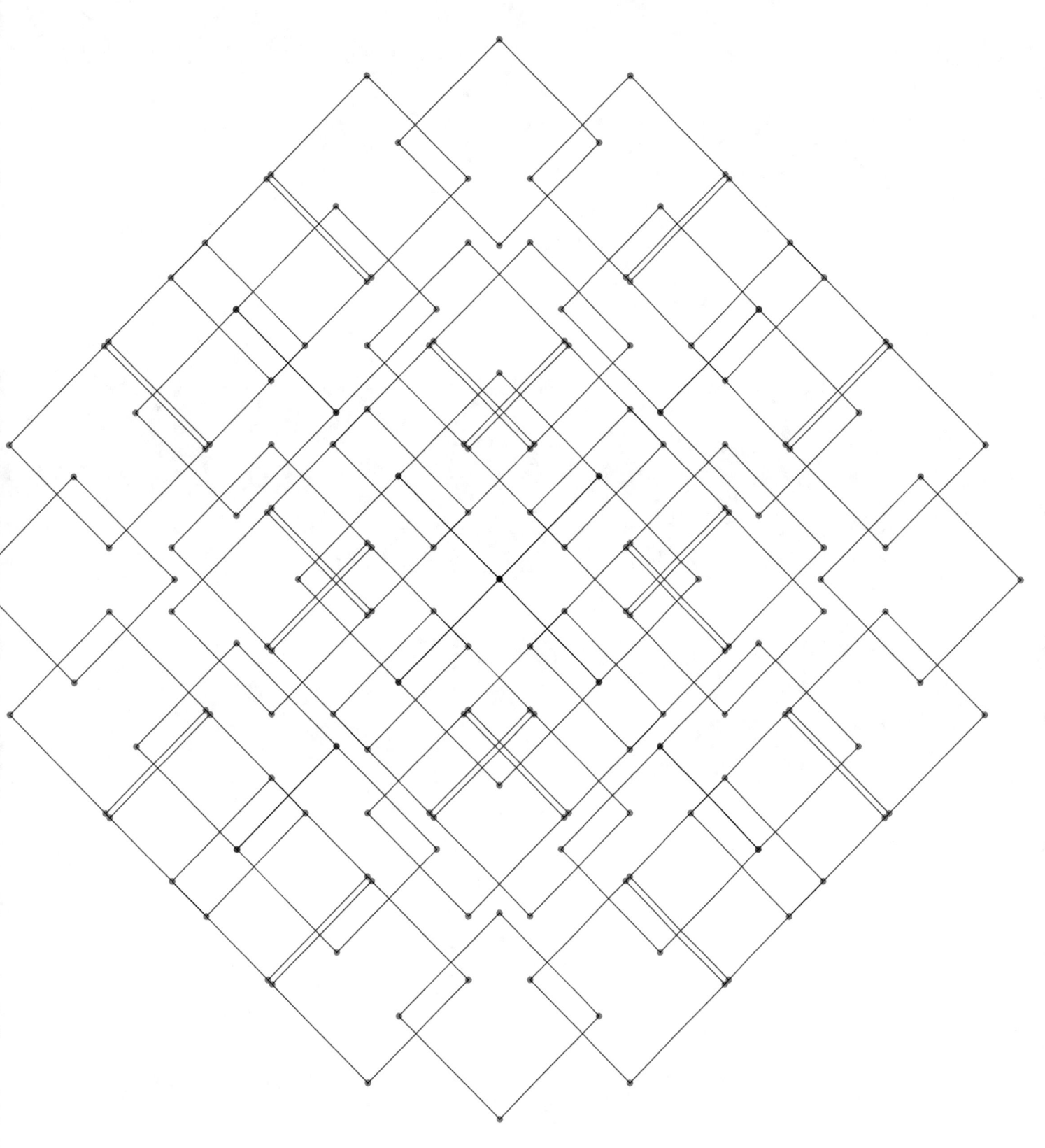

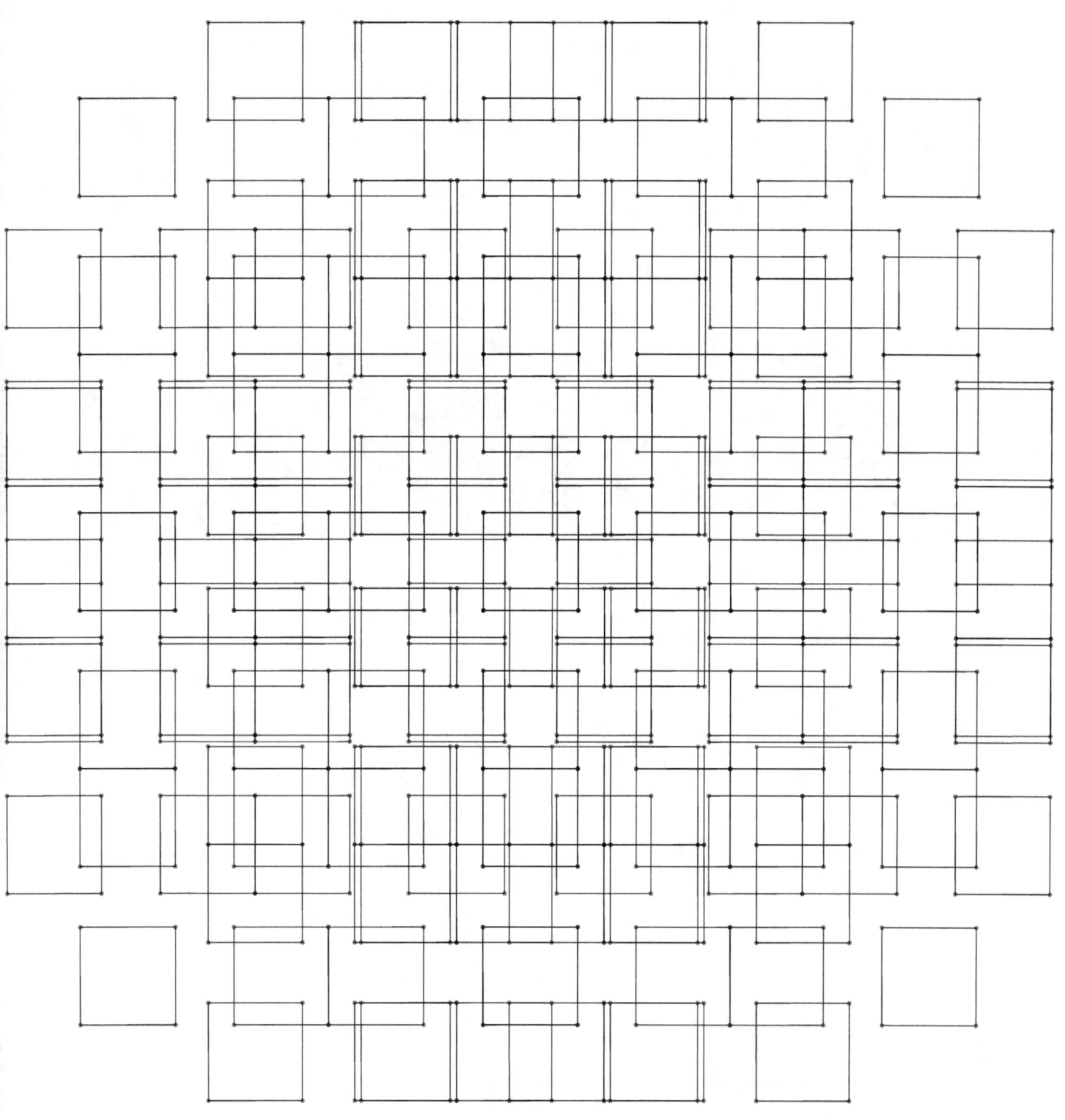

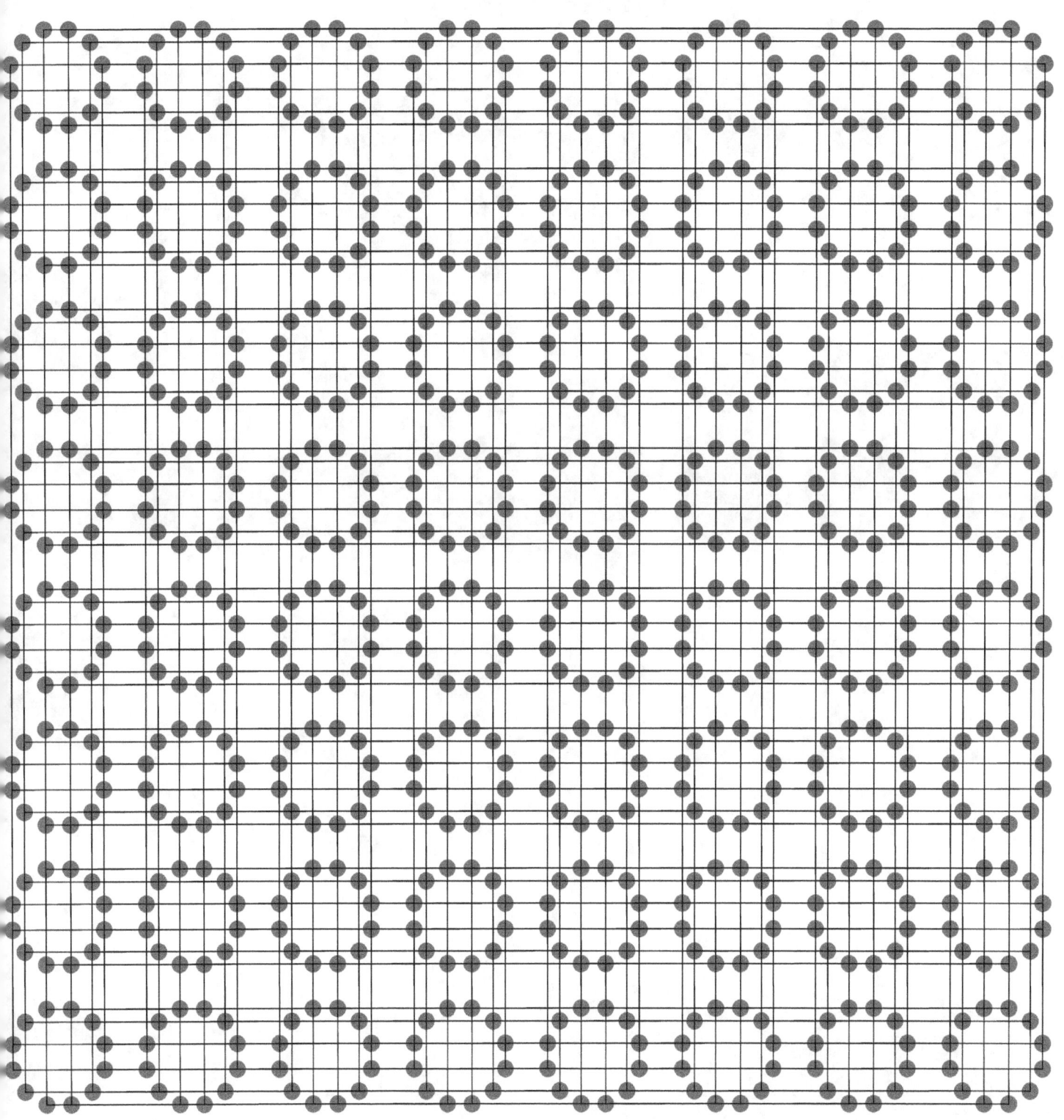

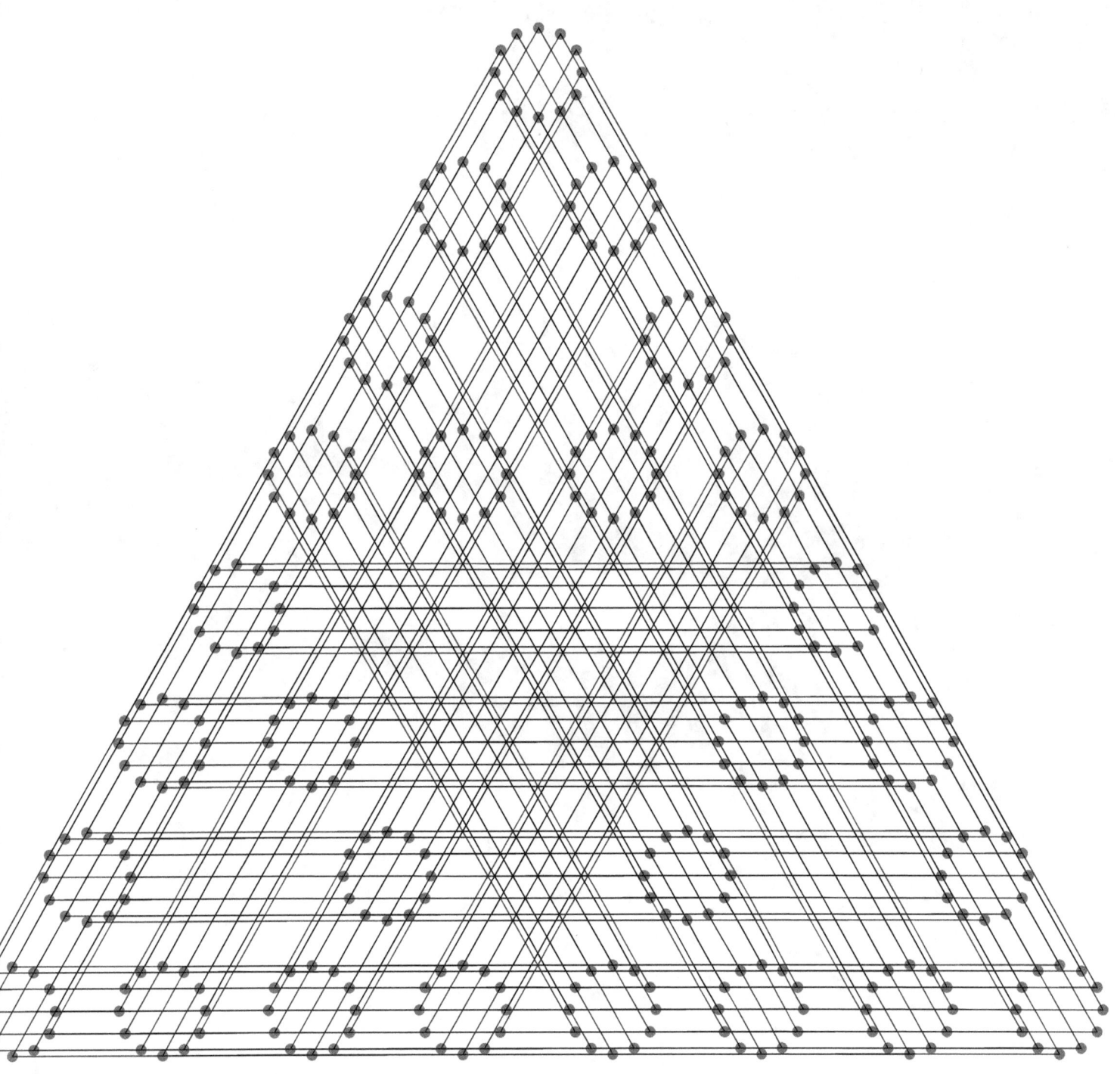

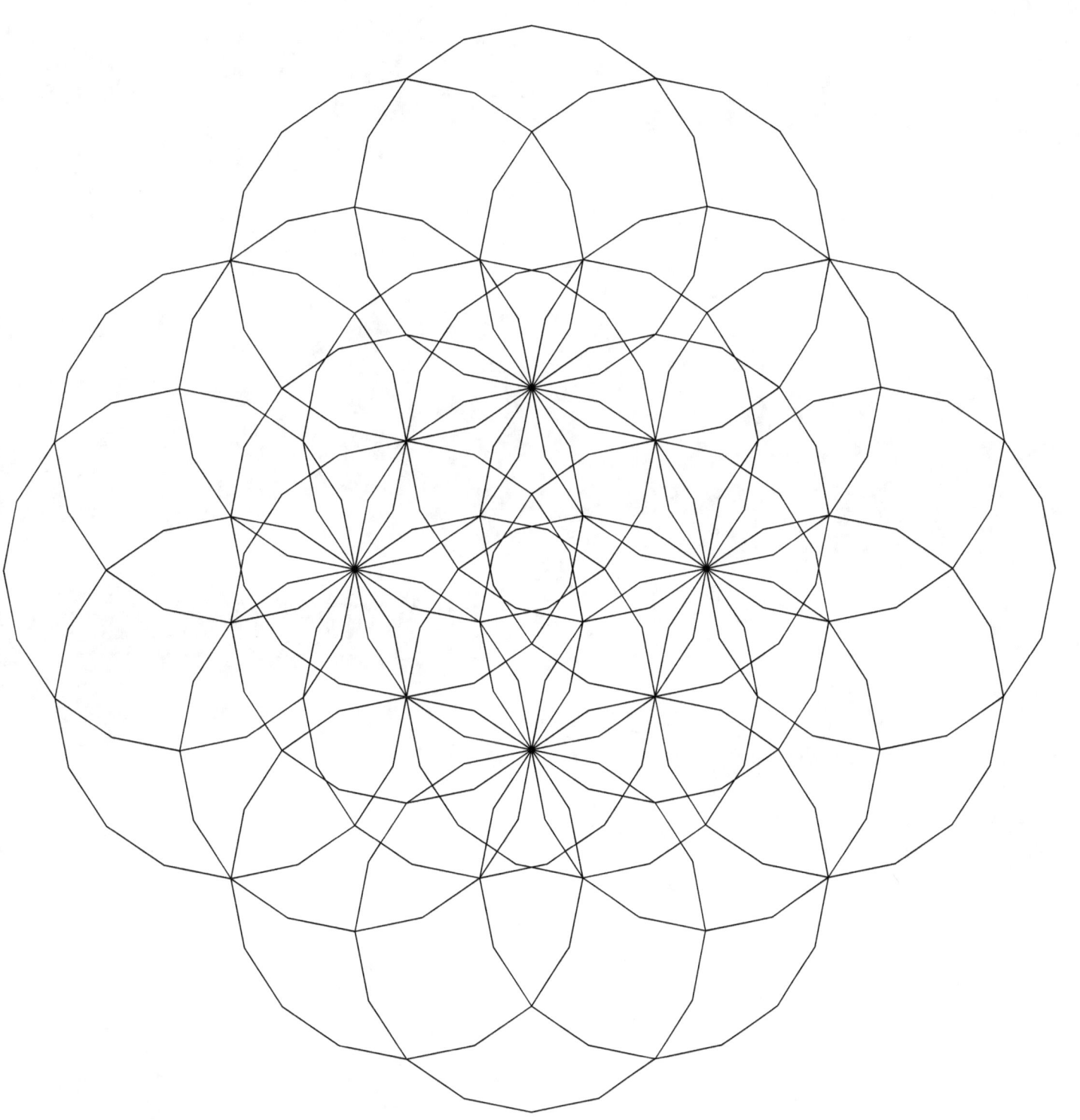

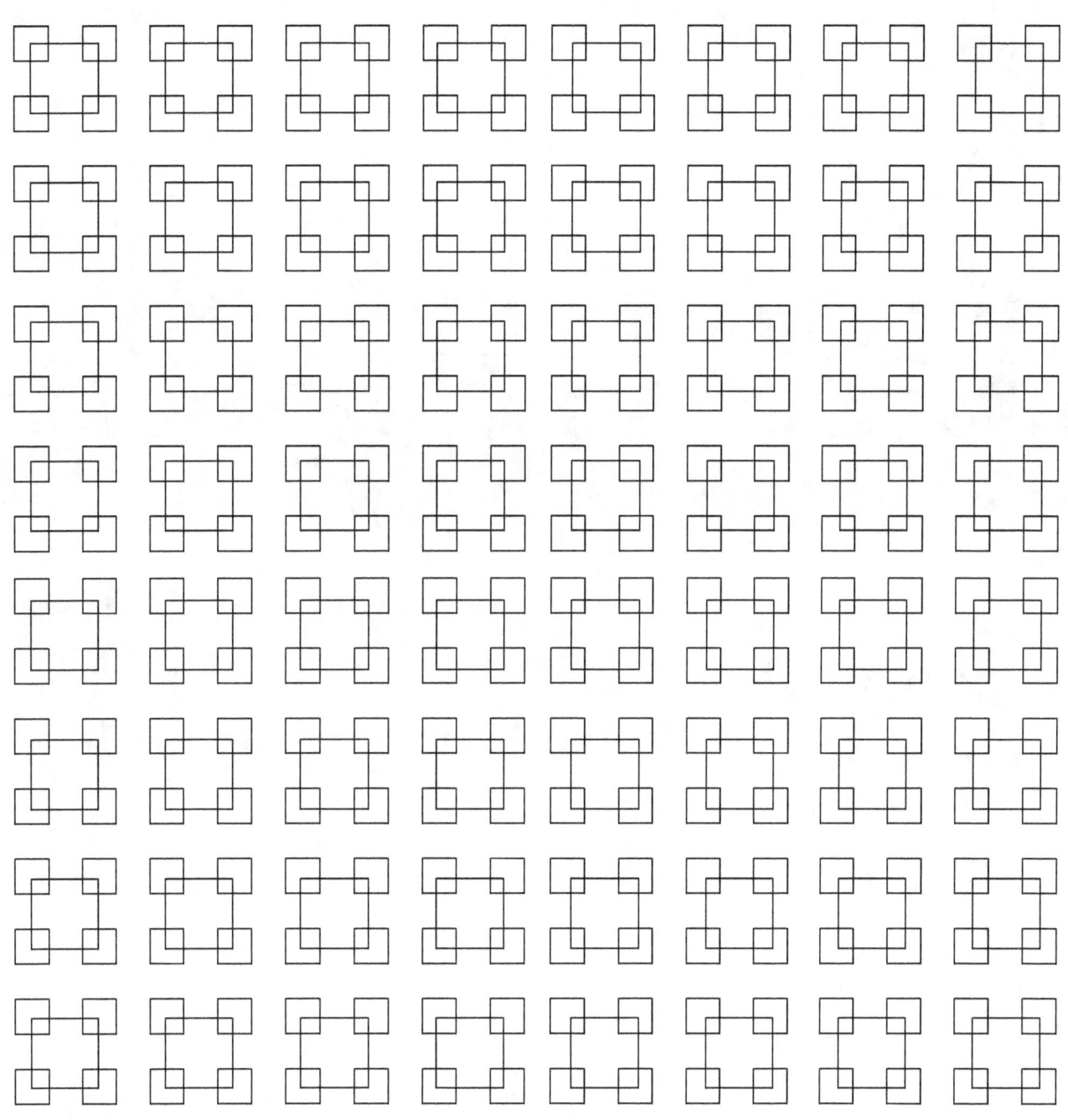

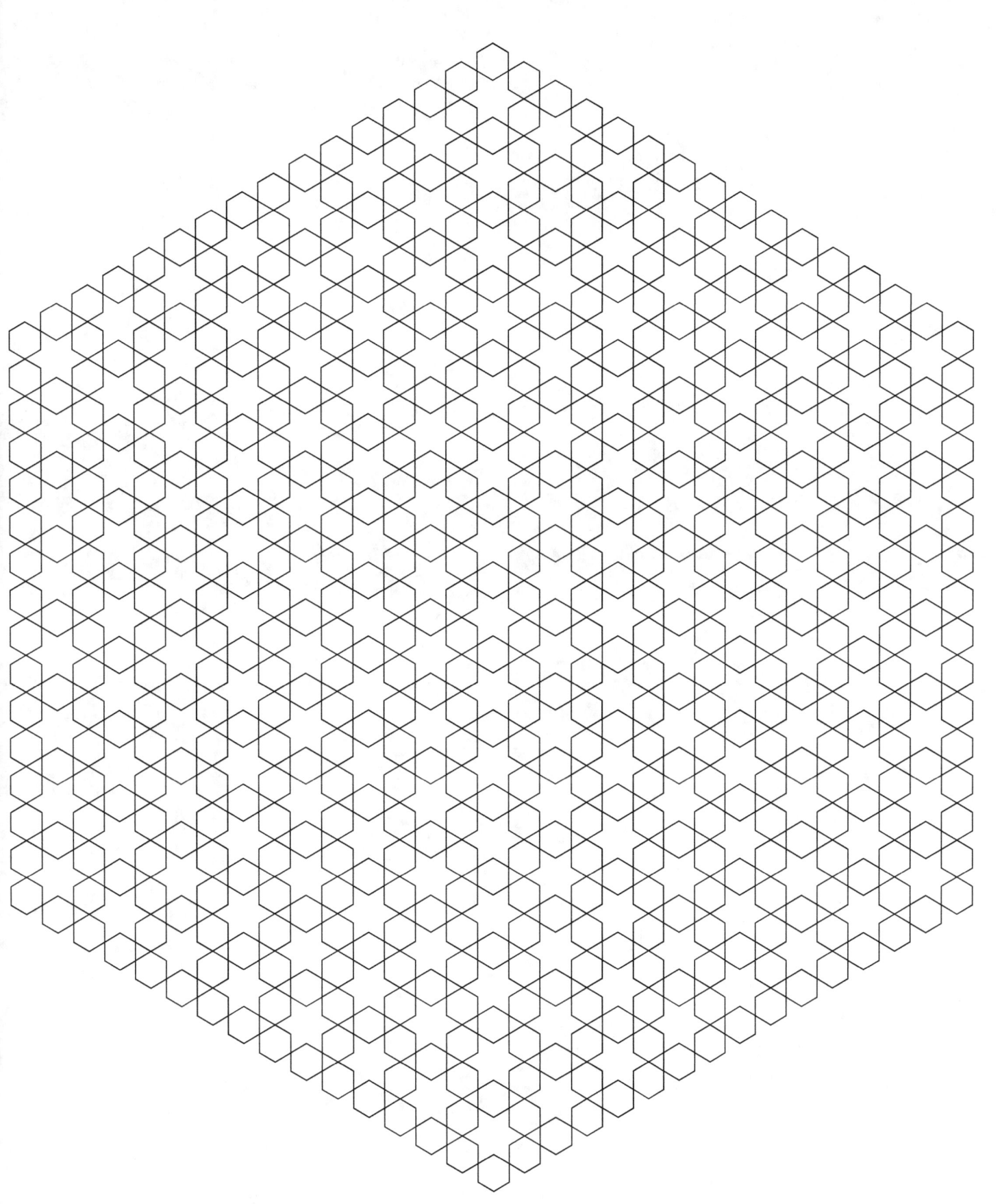

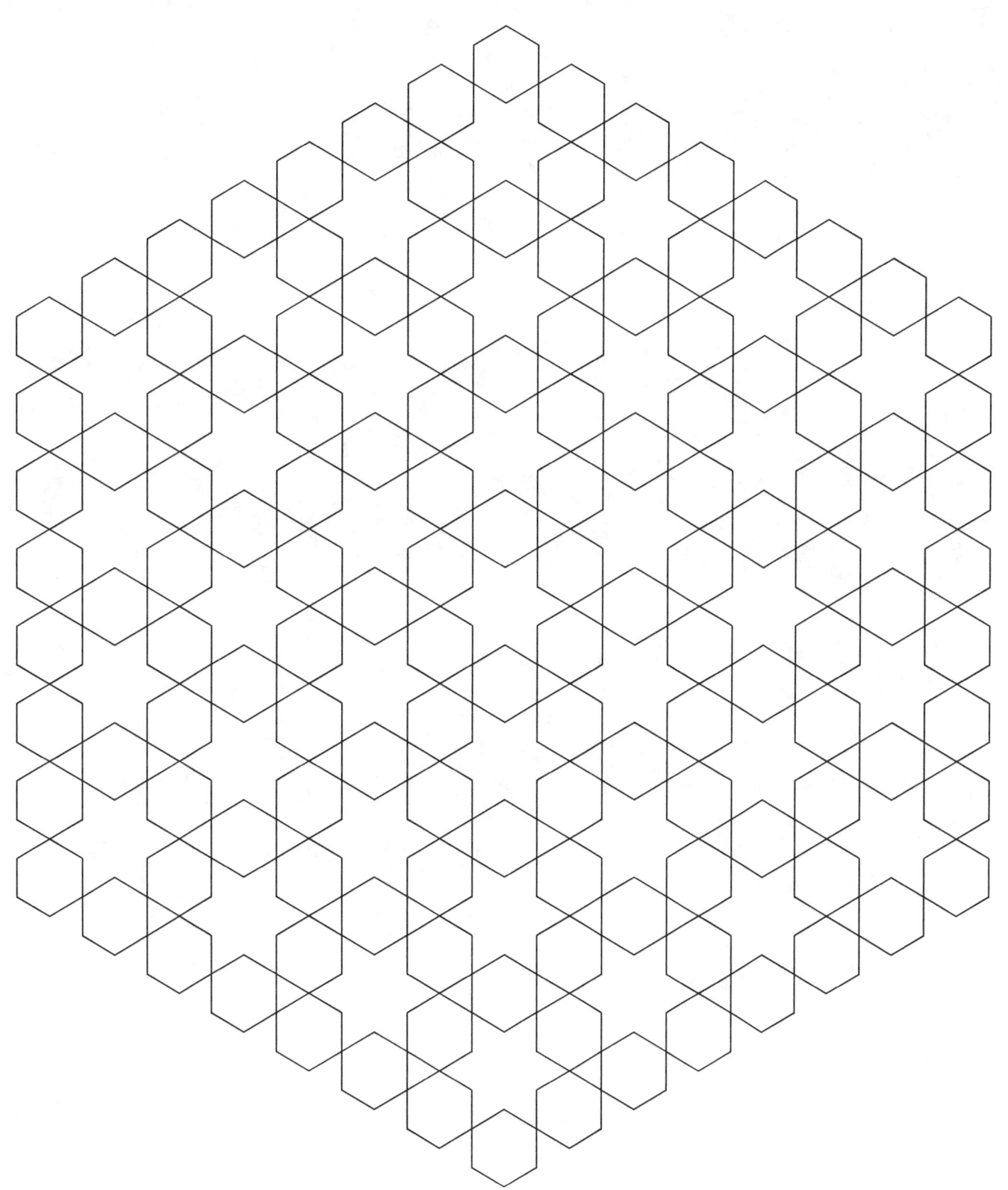

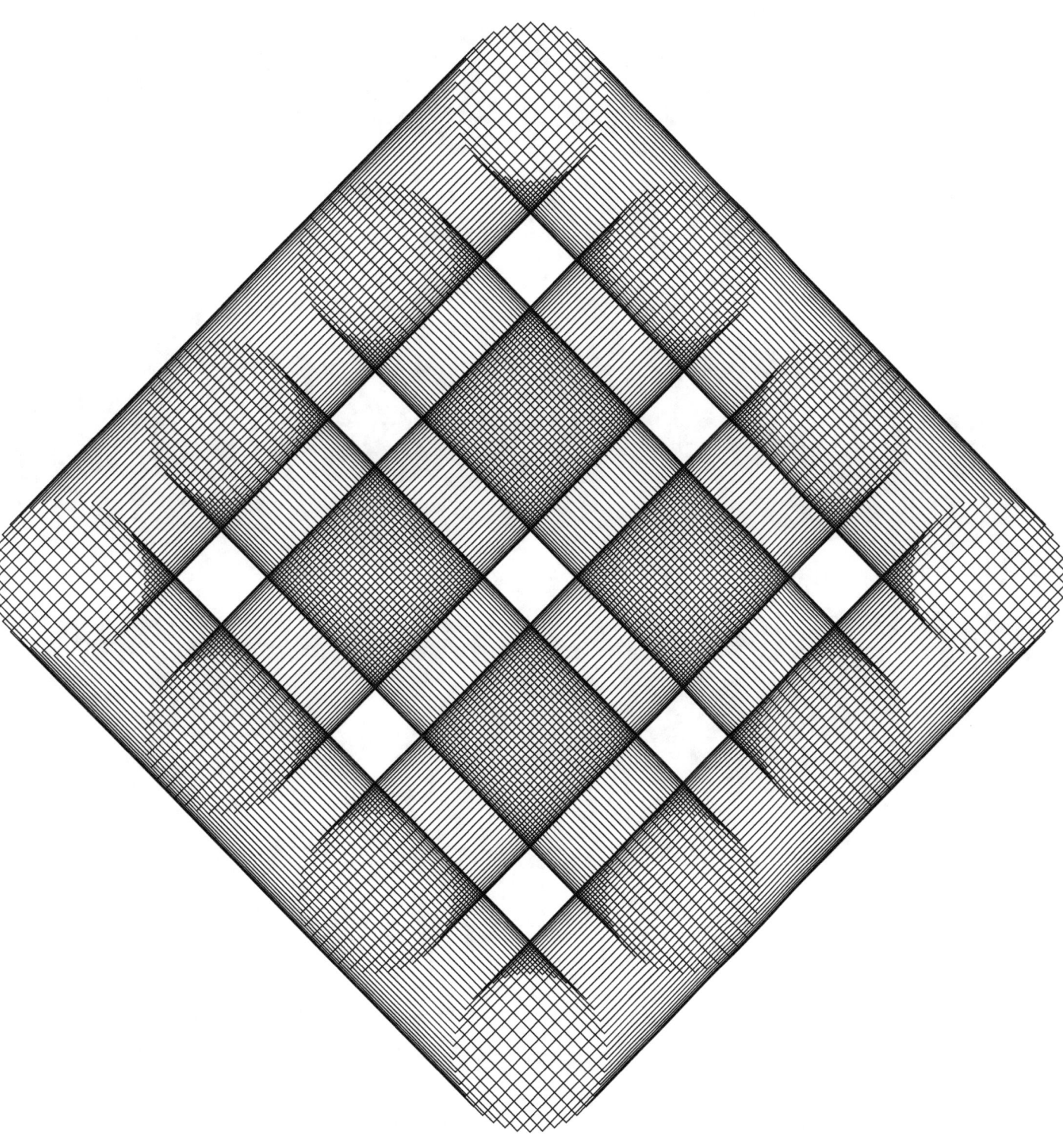

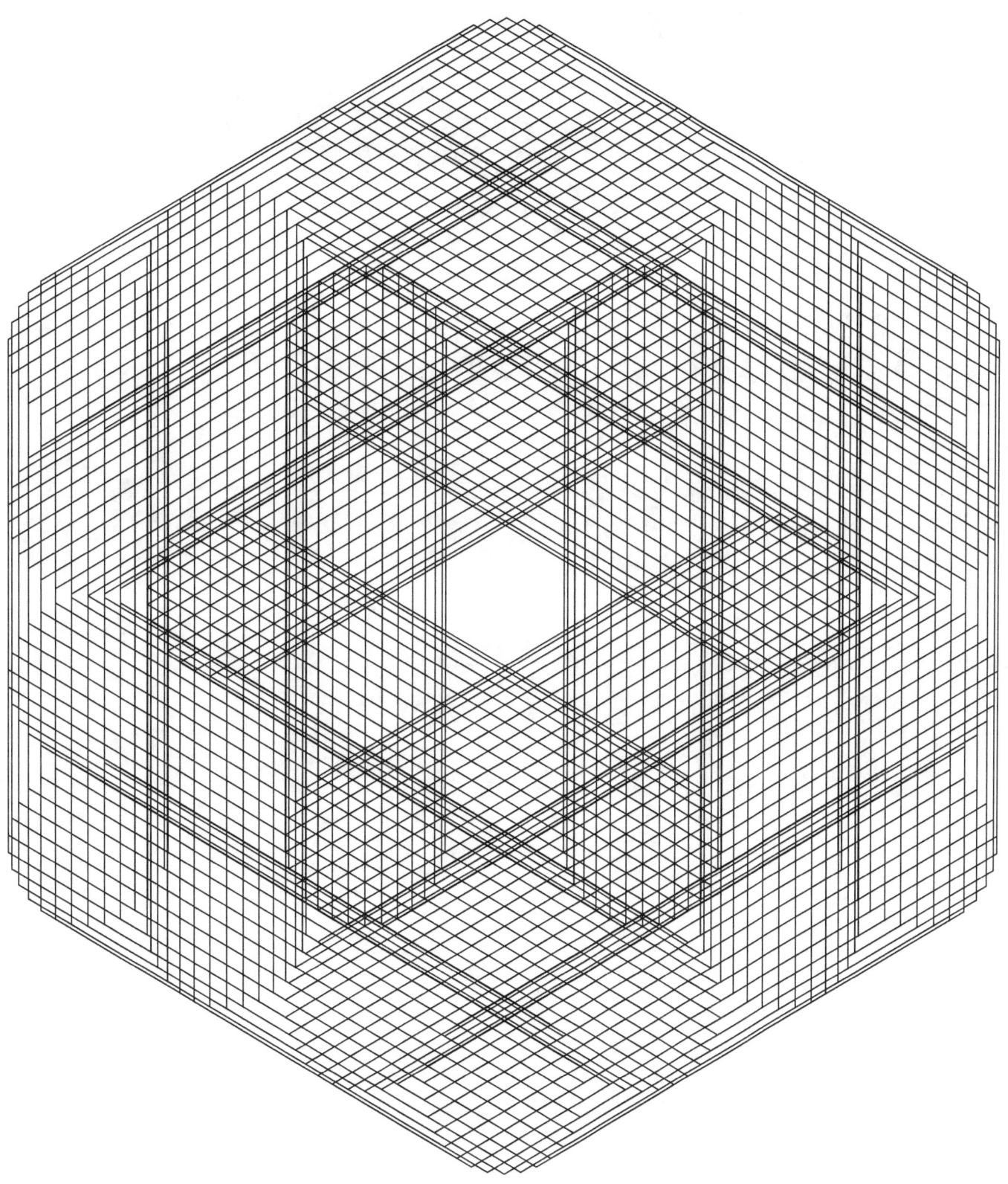

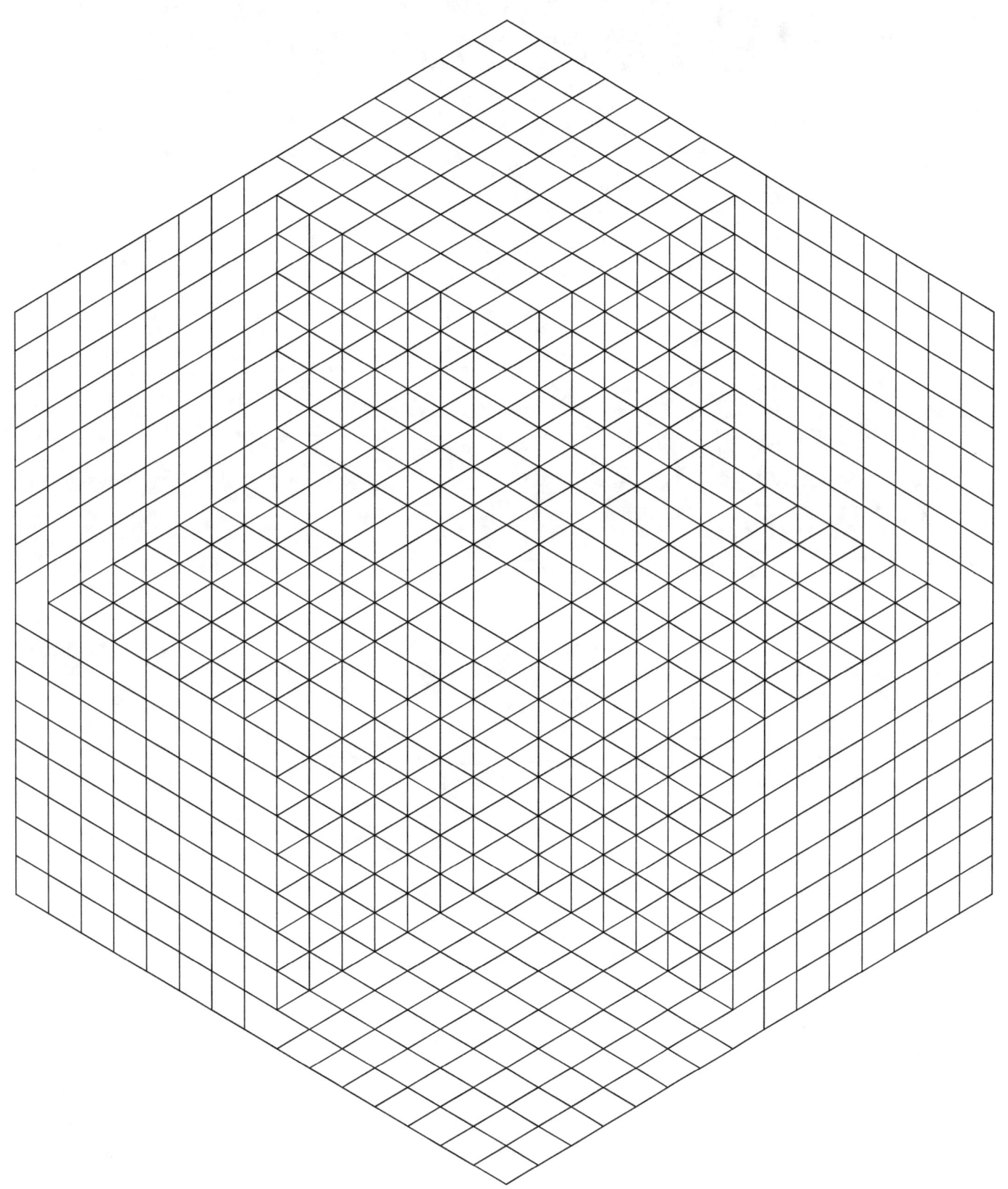

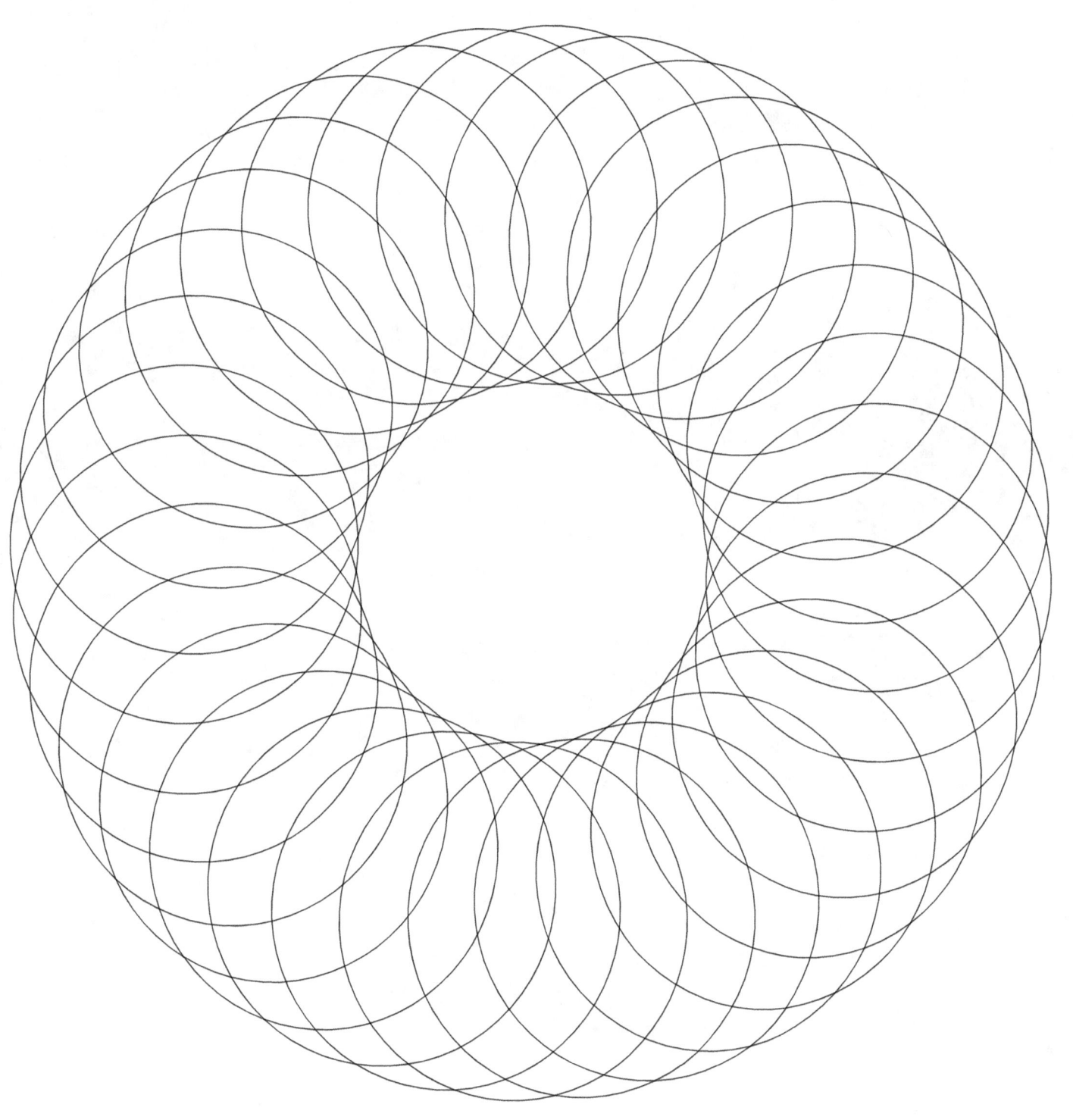

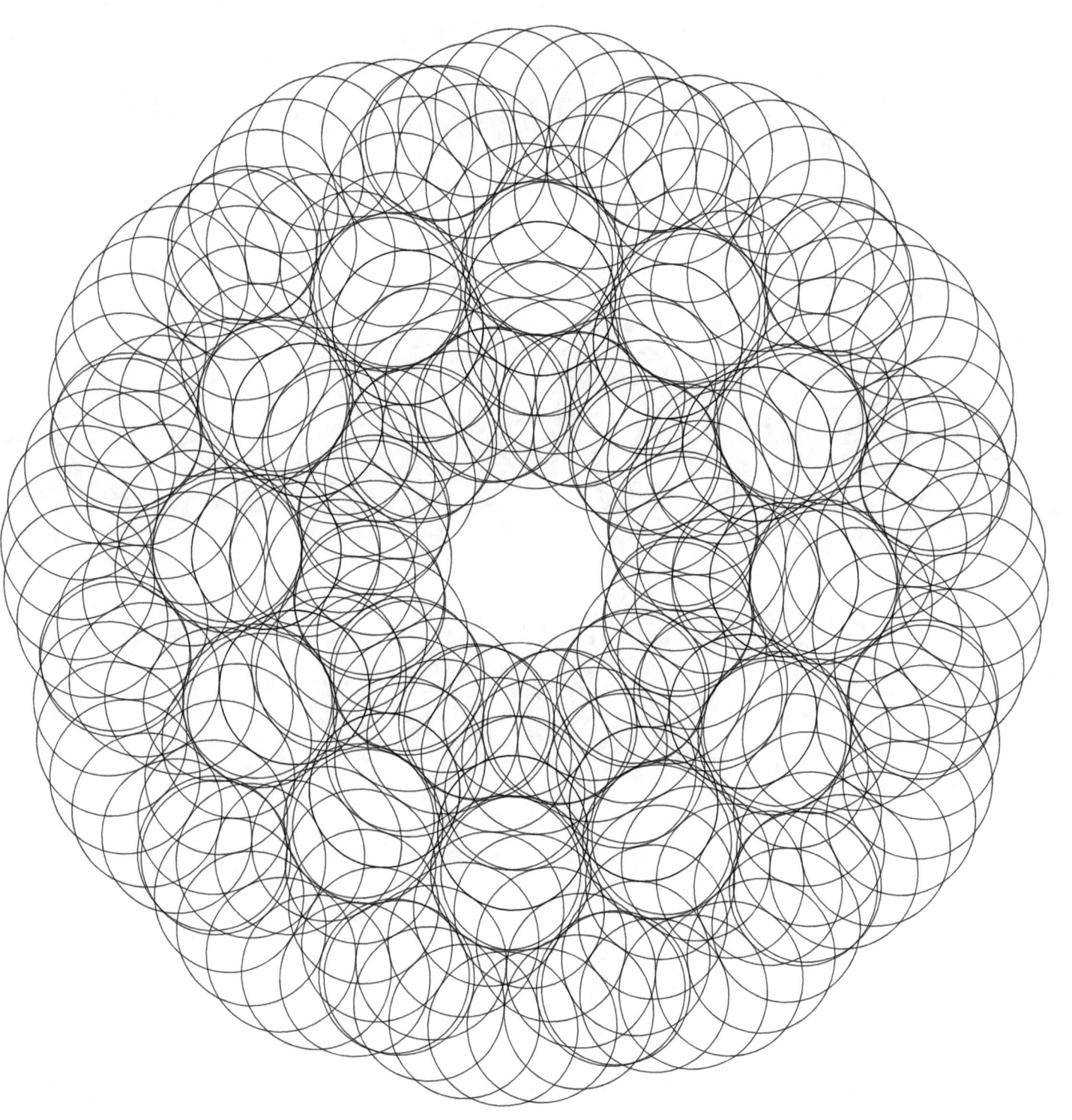

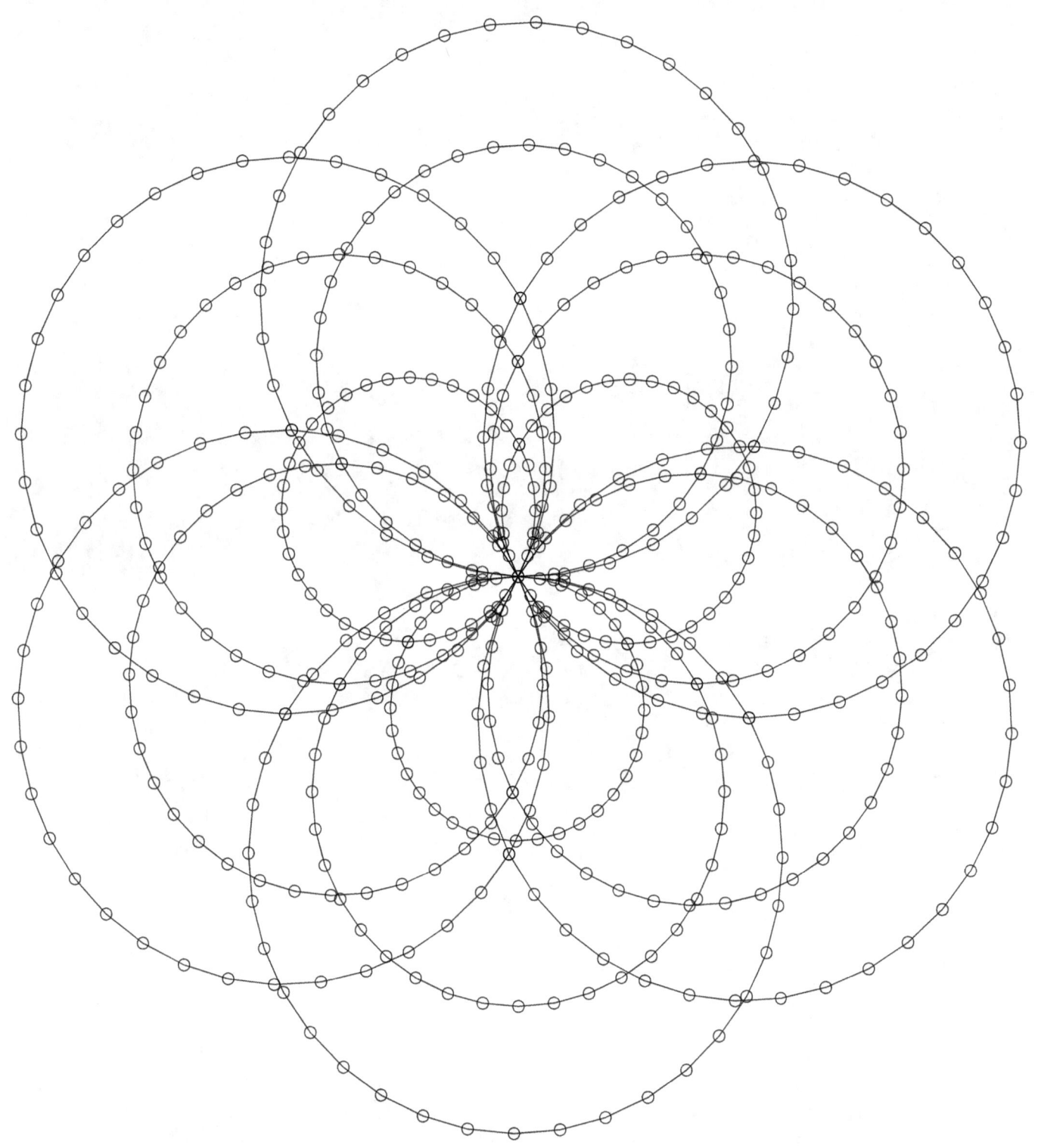

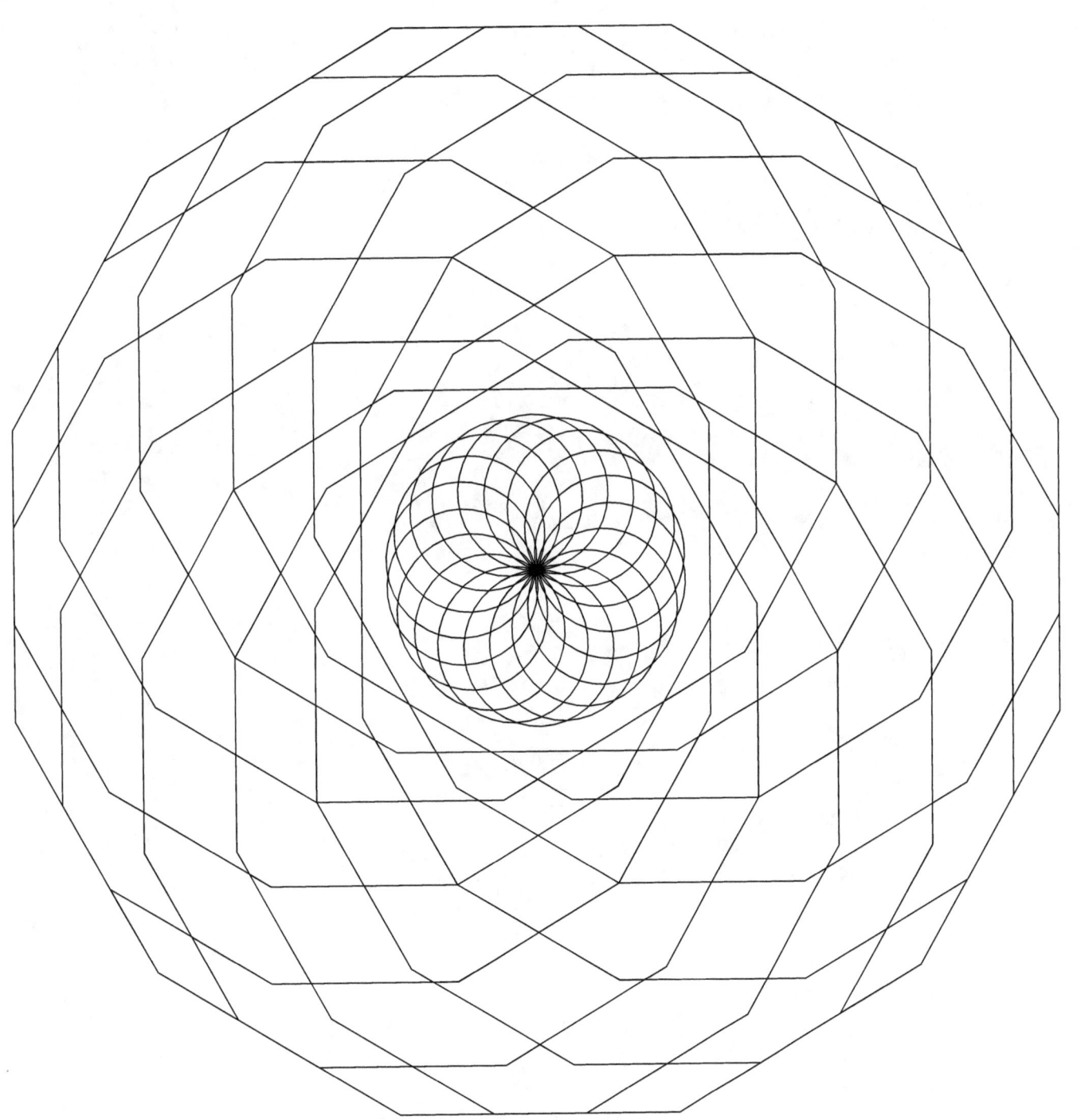

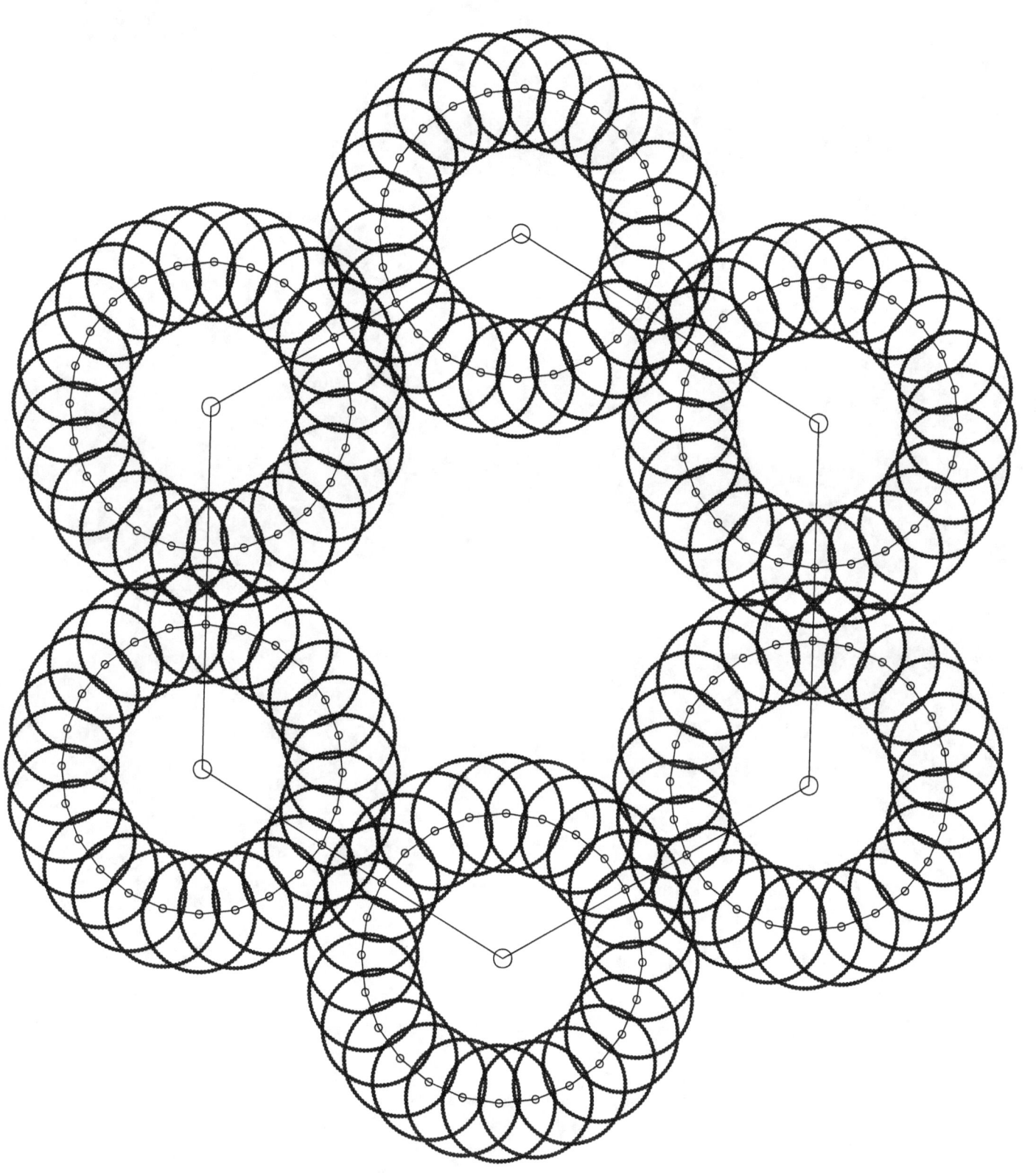

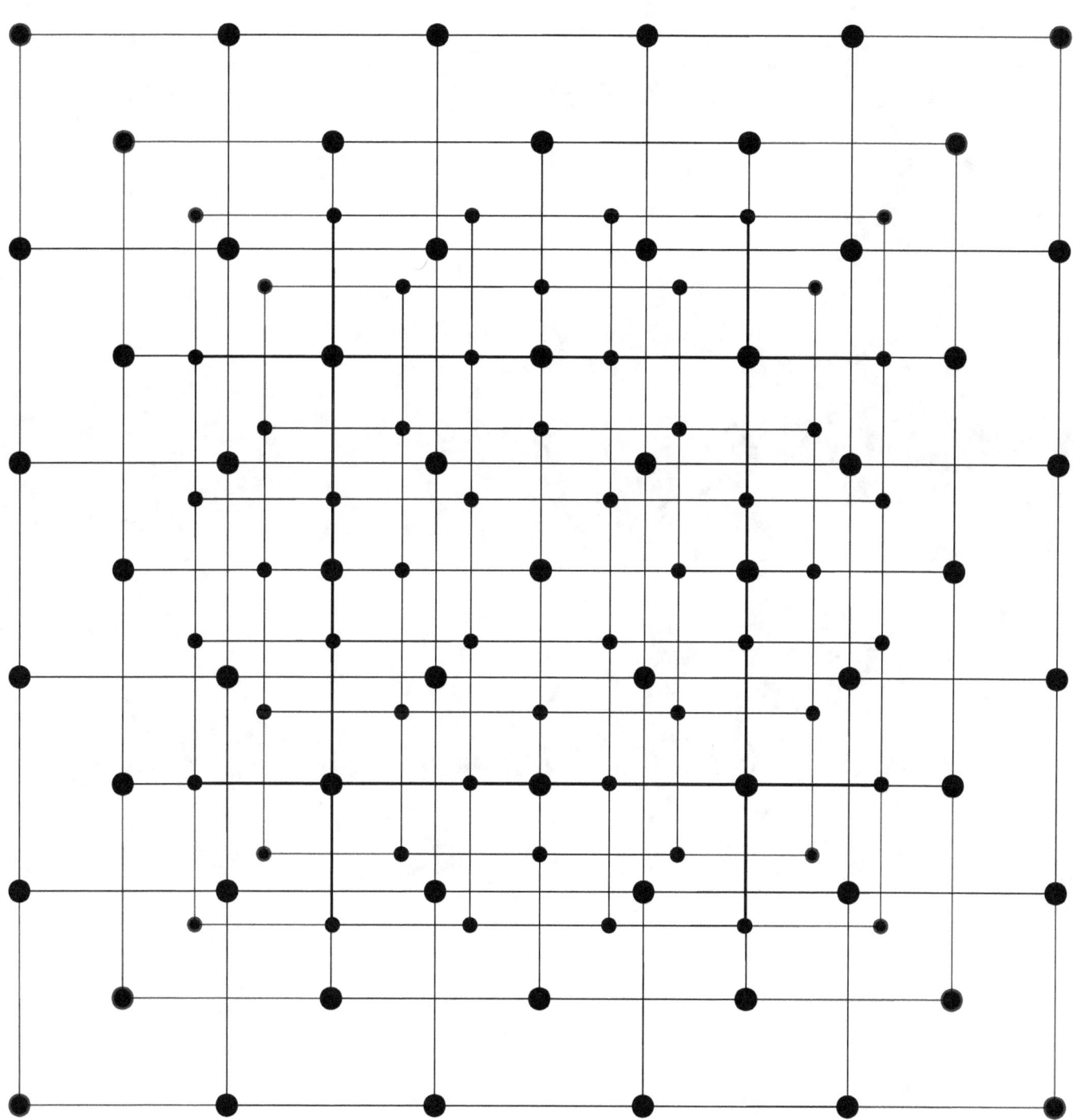

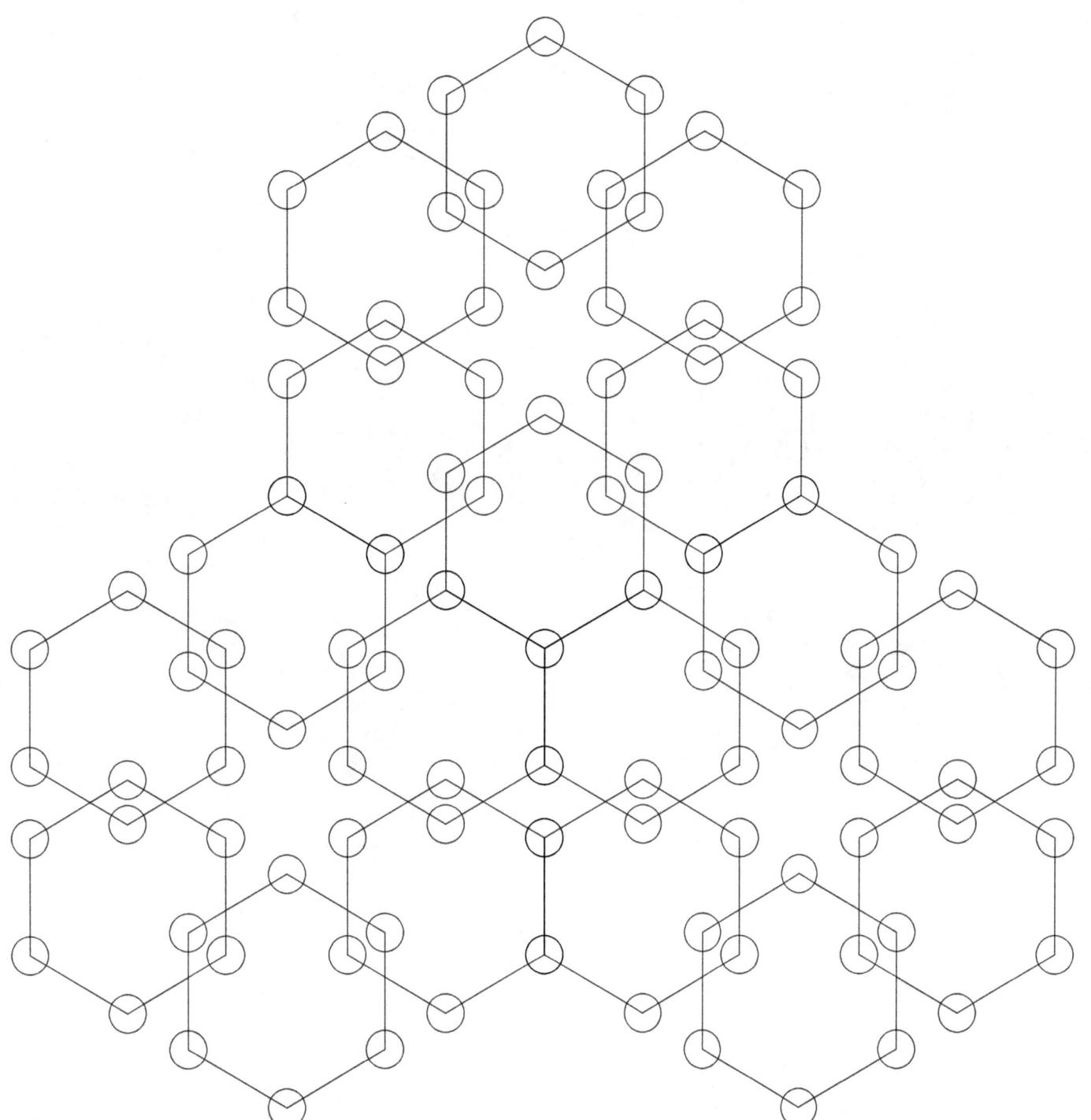

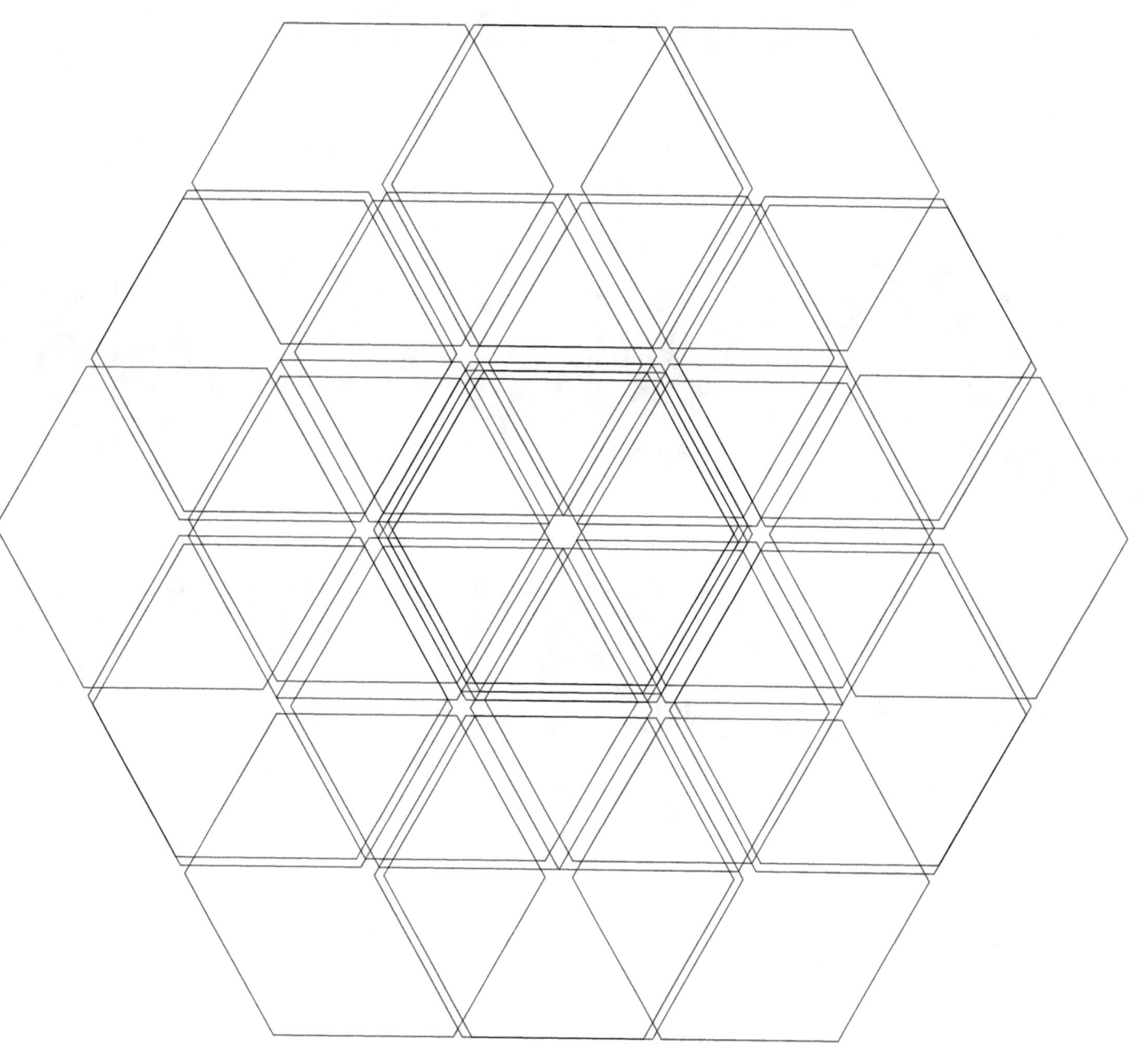

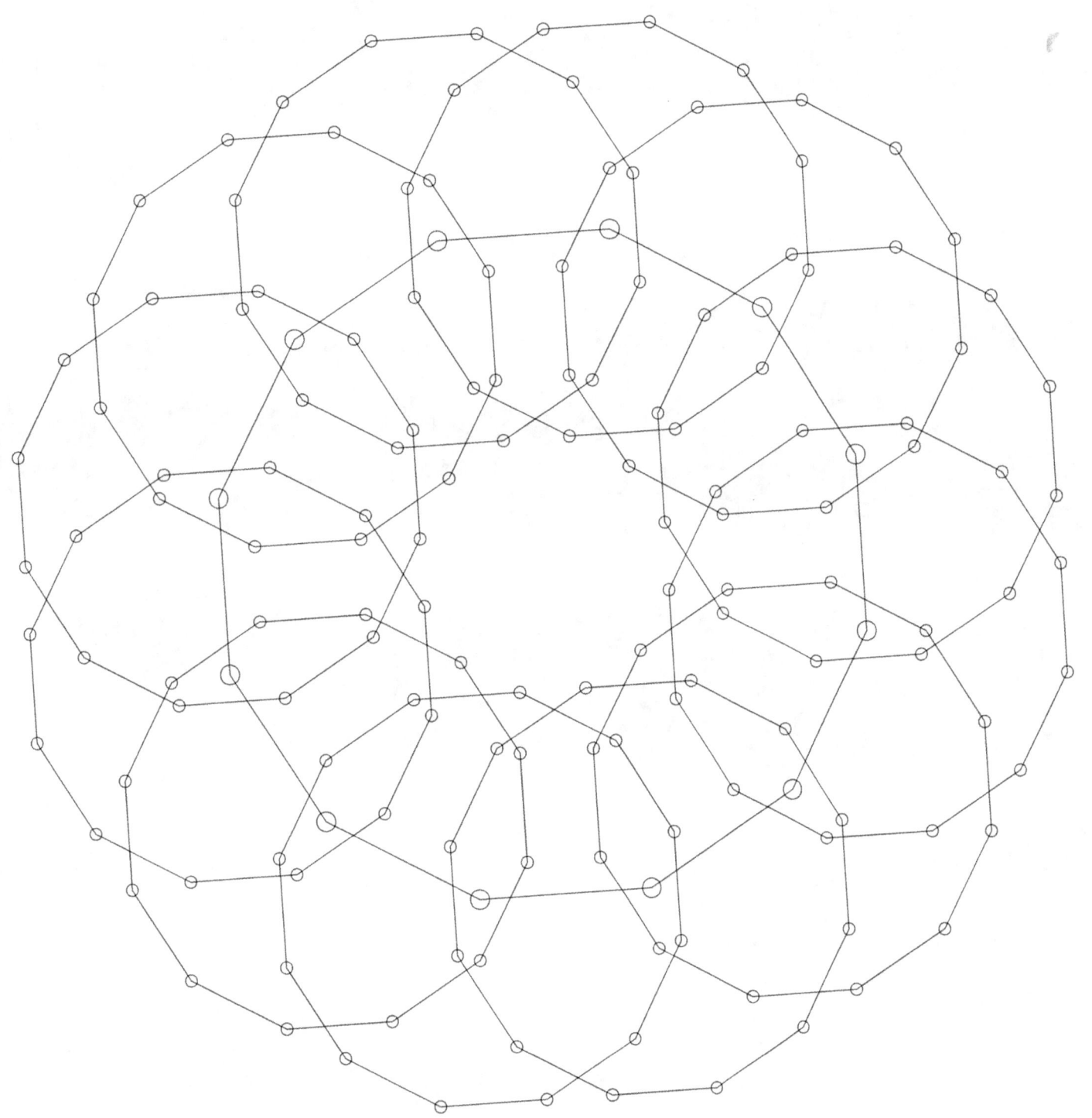